Beyond the Wall

An Anthology of Poetry and Prose

Printed by Anchor Print Group Limited

Published by Anchor Print Group Limited
in assocciation with
Vaughan Writers

May 2013

ISBN: 978-1-907540-87-5

Cover Photo Courtesy of Jack Hargreaves

Introduction to

'Beyond the Wall'

A writer writes ... a simple statement, but it requires willpower, determination and discipline - as well as talent. A pot of glue to secure your backside to the chair might help! In the modern world there are so many distractions and it is much easier to just fantasise about winning the Booker prize. The number of people who glibly remark 'I could write a book ...' but do they? That is why the book you are now holding is such a worthwhile achievement.

Vaughan Writers have worked together since 2002 writing poetry and prose, and now meet in the convivial surroundings of The Belmont Hotel, New Walk, Leicester. They look upon their meetings as a lifeline of support, encouragement and feedback for the sometimes lonely occupation of writing. Individual members have been published, had plays performed, and had success in writing competitions.

To be a writer you must also be a good reader because inspiration can be found from many different sources: Myth pools; Greek drama; the Bible; classical and modern novels and even Mr. Leicester's page in the Mercury! The creation, in poetry and prose, of new worlds of the imagination lie Beyond the Wall and Vaughan Writers hope that you will enter them. Now, read on ...

Contents

THE DAY THE RAIN CAME

Jenny Evans

The day the rain came marked the end of four weeks of stifling heat. The energy sapping humidity was washed away, along with the crusty debris that had littered the streets, and the whole country breathed a huge communal sigh of relief.

In his flat at number 22, Rod stood in the bay window ironing his work shirt and watching water erupt out of a popped drain cover. A half-eaten piece of toast sat on a plate in front of the television. Dragging his attention away from the river that was now running down Cracknell Road, Rod turned to listen to the local news.

Another two shop break-ins during the night. More jewellery gone. No clues to the identity of the thieves. Police are investigating.

"Usual platitudes," he thought to himself.

Back on the street a car pulled up outside the house opposite. Rod watched for a few seconds, but the driver didn't emerge, probably waiting to see if the downpour would ease off a bit. Rod was carefully ironing a sharp crease in his trousers when he saw a movement out the corner of his eye.

The car door opened slightly and an attractive girl carrying a large shoulder bag emerged, and hurriedly put up an umbrella. Her feet were immediately covered by the deluge rushing down the road. Not seeming to care, she waded through the water and onto the pavement. Shaking the wet from her feet, she ran to the porch of her house, and dropped the umbrella to one side.

"Very tasty," Rod thought. He'd watched her arrive home at about the same time several mornings over the last couple of weeks, so he assumed she worked nights. He was just conjuring up a scenario where they would accidentally happen upon each other outside her house, when he saw her turn in his direction.

Realising he was now standing in full view in his bay window, he was about to step back when she looked up at him. He could see the rain dripping from her fringe, and as she pushed her hair back, she met his eyes and smiled at him. He raised his hand in embarrassment, and then moved out of sight, but not before he saw her laughing as she went into the house, closing the front door behind her.

Mortified, he slumped down in front of the television.

"Great," he said, "good job. Now she'll think I'm some bloody peeping tom."

Back on the local news they were showing photos of some of the more unusual pieces of jewellery that had been taken in the recent raids. One pair of earrings were apparently the only ones of their kind. Diamonds set in platinum twists, but mirror images of each other. Police were appealing for anyone who might have seen anything suspicious to come forward. A substantial reward was on offer.

Next was the weather forecast. Rain, rain and more rain seemed to be on the menu for the next few days.

"We need it," Rod thought, "especially the gardens." He groaned out loud. "Oh God. I'm turning into my father."

****

At Redgrave Road Police Station, Rod was finishing his shift. His desk was strewn with photos of the jewellery stolen in the recent robberies and he was trying to get them into some sort of order. He picked up the picture of the earrings that had been shown on the local news. They were certainly beautiful, even Rod's untrained eye could see that, but so distinctive that he doubted anyone would have the nerve to wear them.

"Probably stolen to order," he thought.

Now he'd got promotion to plain clothes he was out and about a lot more, which suited him very well, but still the paperwork seemed endless.

He was a member of an eight man team working on the robberies, and in spite of the police bravado on the television, at the moment they were pretty much stumped.

"Police are investigating, huh," he thought to himself. "More like, police are hoping someone will make a mistake, and they'll get lucky."

Rod put the photos in a filing cabinet and finished his report. Pulling on his jacket he headed towards the door.

"Bye John," he acknowledged the Sergeant at the desk, "You coming to the D&D?"

"Yeh, I'll be there," John replied, "about 8.00."

"Great, see you later then. I'll get them in," and he set off for the walk home.

Normally he would have driven to and from work to save some time, but he'd taken to walking in the hope of bumping into the girl who lived in the house opposite. Although she seemed to work most nights, he'd seen her from his flat window during the day, so he knew she was out and about sometimes.

Their morning wave was turning into a ritual and Rod had decided that it was time to take the potential relationship to the next stage. By chatting to the fount of all knowledge that was Mrs Pinsent, his landlady, he'd managed to find out that the girl's name was Beverley and she didn't appear to have a boyfriend. He was not confident, but hopeful.

Since the day the rain came, which was now over two weeks ago, he and Beverley had smiled and waved to each on a number of mornings. As soon as she arrived home he would put down his iron and go to the window. Then she would climb out of her car, lug her huge designer bag to her doorstep, and turn his way.

Yes, it was definitely time to move to the next stage of the friendship, if there was going to be one.

****

Rod and Beverley were sitting in the corner of the Dog and Duck, both drinking pints of Speckled Hen. The first time they had gone to the pub Rod had been surprised that Beverley had ordered a pint. Even now that he was used to it, it still surprised him.

They touched glasses, "Cheers," she said.

"Cheers," he replied. "Still don't think you look like a pint drinker. Much too feminine."

"Oh I'm a lot tougher than I look," she replied. "Had to be with my upbringing. Five older brothers to keep me on my toes. They taught me everything I know, that's why I'm so streetwise."

"Better watch my step then," Rod laughed, "Five knights in shining armour ready to defend your honour at the drop of a crisp packet."

Beverley laughed with him. "Yes, you're right. Many a potential boy friend has been frightened off, thanks to them. But I have a feeling that you're made of sterner stuff."

"Let's hope so. I'll do my best." Rod studied her face as she looked round the bar. She really was very pretty, but not in a conventional way, more quirky. This was the third time they'd been out and he was beginning to feel that there might be something brewing between them. There was still a lot to know about each other, in fact this was the first time that Beverley had mentioned her family, but they had lots of time to delve a bit deeper.

He still hadn't got to the bottom of what job she did. All she would say was that it was part-time work and all a bit boring. Some sort of care worker he assumed. He also hadn't yet told her that he was a policeman, as it sometimes put people off. He just said he worked in the community.

Tonight she was wearing a purple mini dress, over leggings and long black boots. Very tasty she looked, and was getting more than a few admiring glances from the men round the bar. When John and his wife left the pub earlier, he had given Rod an exaggerated wink, as if to say "you lucky bugger."

Her long hair, which was normally hanging loose, was tonight tied forward in braids, knotted with ribbons. "Very hippy chick," he thought. She was having problems with it though. Every time she took a sip of beer she dunked the ends of her hair in the sticky liquid.

"Oh I'm fed up with this," she said eventually. Then proceeded to unravel the ribbon from her hair. Soon it was back to its normal style, apart from the kinks left from the braiding. "That's better," she said.

Whilst she'd been sorting her hair out, Rod had been frantically racking his brains. He'd seen something, but he wasn't sure what.

"You ok?" Beverley asked, "You seem a bit distracted."

"I'm fine thanks, just trying to remember, I'm not sure what."

"Well you have a little think, and I'll go and get another drink. Same again?"

"Thanks." Rod watched as she ordered the beers, paid for them and made her way back to the table.

"There you go. Well have you remembered?" she asked as she sat down again.

Rod leaned towards her. Taking her face in his hands and gently pushing her hair back from her face, he moved forward as if to kiss her. She half closed her eyes and leaned towards him expectantly.

"Those really are lovely earrings," he said, "and extremely distinctive."

THE ITALIAN RENAISSANCE

Ann Fuchs

Merely glancing at the elegant displays of shoes and clothes, she walked briskly to the restaurant. It was dark and the only light came from the shop windows. People strolled in groups. Even on this frost cold night, chatting and laughing, men and women sauntered as they would on a warm summer's evening. She admired the capacity of the Italians to chat endlessly and with such passion. But it was a passing thought as she dwelt on her meeting with David. His phone call had brought back memories which swamped her with the conflicting feelings of love and hate.

The restaurant was along a dark alleyway where cafes, lit with tiny white lights, nestled at the base of high buildings. The wind was sharp. She quickened her pace, pulling her coat collar up to her neck.

It appeared full and she could not see David amongst the faces that turned towards her. The air was warm with smells of garlic and wine. The warmth of the atmosphere was echoed in the red table cloths and napkins.

'Joanna.'

She turned to see him seated in a room adjacent, alone at a table by the window.

This small room was empty of other diners.

'David.'

And thirty years melted into insignificance. She began to feel nervous. She wanted to start again. See him at the wedding tomorrow and then, if all went well, perhaps meet for dinner. At that moment she regretted she had agreed to meet.

'What an amazing coincidence', he kissed her on either cheek.

'Not really. You do remember we were both asked to be godparents.'

'Of course, but you may have decided not to attend the wedding. Or I could have had business on the other side of the world. So, perhaps it's not amazing, but you have to admit, it's just wonderful.'

She sat opposite him. She felt uncomfortable as he scrutinised her face. Oh God, he still has that innate charm. He can still insinuate himself into her world. Hair greying and solidly built, he looked glossy and prosperous.

'I think we should have some Prosecco first. This is the start of a weekend of celebrations. Where are you staying? At the Hotel Baglione?'

'Yes.'

'That's good. I can walk you back. I'm also booked in there. Oh, it's so good to see you and you haven't changed. Your lips are just as I remember them. I could …'

'David. Please.'

Two women walked into the room; both blond and pretty, one younger than the other. They sat at a table further away but it seemed close because of the size of the room. They didn't speak to each other. David looked up and smiled at them. He had always been friendly and open. They did not notice. Their faces had the closed look of anger or discomfort.

'Well, who will start. We have a lot of ground to catch up. Sorry that sounds so business-like.' He laughed.

'Oh, so I'm being fitted in between business meetings. Tout ca change, tout c'est la meme chose.' Joanna reacted as she had done in the past when their relationship fell apart.

David smiled.

'Joanna, please. I am sorry. I'm so eager to hear how you are and what you are doing. If I sound insensitive, please forgive me.'

They ordered the food. David's Italian sounded impeccable. He was an archetypal European.

'I really am not happy about the situation'. The older blond woman spoke clearly in a moderated American accent. Joanna turned to look at her. Her face was set in disapproval.

'Mom, I'm sorry but you will have to meet him before you say that.'

'Joanna, where are you? Cheers, bon chance and here's to a fun weekend. Do you know who else from the group is coming to the wedding?'

'Sorry, David.' And lowering her voice, 'have you noticed those two Americans?'

Mother and daughter not getting on well at all. I guess it's a problem over the boyfriend.'

'Still people watching?'

'Yes.'

Two men took the table next to them. Both pale and fat with grey cropped hair. One wore steel rimmed glasses which reminded Joanna of her professor of French at Cambridge.

'Joanna!' David's voice sharply caught her attention, 'we have not seen each other for years. How many? And you find the other diners more interesting.'

'Oh, I'm so sorry. It's the habit of a life time. I do find people fascinating.'

'But not me'.

'Yes, and you'. But I'm anxious, she thought.

She took a long drink of wine. This gave her the opportunity to think how to turn the conversation onto neutral ground. The wine started to relax her. The pasta arrived and David ordered a bottle of Chianti.

'It's not as though we have to drive. The Hotel is magnificent isn't? My room has the most delightfully carved wooden ceiling, very Tuscan. Geoffrey always liked his comfort. I knew he would choose a classy hotel. Have you seen him lately? I've been abroad so much and when I'm in England I have to see the family.'

The young American woman suddenly stood up and looking down at her mother she spoke quietly and deliberately. Joanna turned to see her throw some money onto the table and leave the room. The older woman opened her bag and coolly gathered the money into her purse. Her actions were measured. It was difficult for Joanna to know whether she was upset or that this was a normal occurrence in her relationship with her daughter. Stop this conjecture. She knew she was engaged in displacement activity. It was easier to be a voyeur than to explore her own feelings, sitting with David. How she had loved him.

'Dear Geoffrey. Yes, we see him and Teresa about two or three times a year. We always talk about our days in Cambridge. But I've hardly seen Emmie.

I always had this romantic idea of being the good godmother and meeting her for lunch in London and going to the theatre. Sadly, it has never happened. I don't suppose you would have the same opportunity. When are you returning to England for good?'

'Soon. I'm taking early retirement. The package is too good to ignore. I can then have a change of direction and resurrect my old friends. Starting with you. How's Tom?'

'Well, happy and older. Busy finishing his book. Deadlines you know. Did we ever think in those days that we would grow old? No, I think mortality was the only subject we didn't discuss.'

'Don't talk like that. We have so much to do yet. Sarah is settled in the family home with a new man. The boys are working. Now I want some time for me, and maybe you?'

Joanna stared at him in wonder. He had left her broken hearted. He had sent an annual Christmas card to her and Tom, and now was he really suggesting that he could resume their relationship which had floundered so many years ago. She decided to ignore the remark.

'What is wrong with the people in this room. The American women were arguing and now those two men behind you appear to be bickering. The one with the glasses has just said he hoped that he was not tiring his friend. How odd or maybe I should say queer.'

As she spoke the words softly and confidentially, looking at David, she saw the flash of irritation cool the warm sparkle which had been in his eyes.

'Sorry, I had forgotten. No, ……it was a Freudian slip. I could never forget. Finishing our relationship was devastating enough, but to be dumped for a man was bloody unpleasant.'

She must have raised her voice as she became aware that their fellow diners had stopped talking and eating.

'It still hurts, doesn't it?'

'Yes, seeing you again like this, the memories are so clear.'

'Darling, Joanna …'

'Don't use terms of endearment when you don't mean it.'

'But I do mean it. I have done a lot of thinking since I divorced Sarah. I know I hurt you. It was a long time ago. I was going through an experimental stage. I wanted to experience everything and I deeply regret what I did to you.'

'So it has taken thirty years. Too late, too late.'

Now Joanna was oblivious to the other diners. She didn't notice the young couple sitting down beside the two men and then after studying the menu, getting up and walking out, gesticulating. The American woman also departed. All these people had now become shadows, a mere backdrop to the intense emotional conversation between them.

'Are you and Tom happy? Does he really love you to distraction? Does he make your life exciting?'

'I tasted the exciting life.'

'What do you mean?'

'You gave me excitement. You showed me passion. I was hooked. It was like a drug. I could never get enough of you, and then after giving myself to you totally. When you saw into my soul. When you had my entire body. You turned from me to that evil manipulative queen. Can you imagine how I felt? Betrayed, soiled. You had opened me up and looked right into me and then you thought you would experiment a little. I don't know what I'm doing here.' She stood up.

'When I heard you were also coming to the wedding I thought about cancelling the trip. I should not have agreed to see you. Oh David, I do feel just as raw as I did all those years ago.'

David reached for her hand as he too stood up.

'Wait. We need to talk. I'll pay the bill.'

The Ponte Vecchio was dark. Lined by tiny jewellery shops now shuttered, hiding their rich dazzling wares. It felt almost menacing. Reminiscent of the days of the Medicis where there was intrigue and murder in each dark shadow. David and Joanna reached the centre of the bridge, stopped and looked down at the river glistening in the moonlight. The black reflections of the houses in the still water would be there in colour tomorrow when the sun will shine, Joanna thought as she stood apart from David. She was standing next to a man whom she had known so intimately all those years ago and now she was frightened of touching him. She was fearful of those powerful emotions enveloping her, making her passionate and irrational once more. David stood, pensively looking down at the water.

'It's too cold to stay here.'

'Yes, I want to return here tomorrow with you and remember the last time we were together.'

'In the cold light of day, we will remember. Will that help me, David?'

'I don't know, but let's try. I've thought a lot about you and we need to reconcile the past.' He sounded tired. His energy dissipated.

They did not see each other at breakfast. Each had decided to have room service. They had arranged to meet in a little café close to the Uffizi. A place they had frequented when David and Joanna were at language school during a summer vacation. They were ecstatic that they had managed to be on the course together. The summer passed in a whirl of culture and totally engrossing love. Joanna knew that this magical time could never be replicated but she had expected their love for each other to continue and mature into a lasting relationship and marriage.

They returned to Cambridge in the October full of anticipation for their final year. Life spread before them full of golden interludes and opportunities.

It was Tom's school friend who had arrived as a fresher. John was a beautiful young man who managed to worm his way into the group. In his way he played with everyone's emotions. Teresa fell for his charms and Geoffrey hated him. He especially sought out David's company whenever he could. Within the two months of the Michaelmas Term, John had managed to drive a wedge between David and Joanna and the final break came in the New Year when David admitted to his attraction to John.

Joanna folded and bowed like a limp tree. She grew thin and angular and cared little for her appearance allowing her fair curls to fall into greasy ringlets. It was Tom who gently brought her back to life over the remaining academic year, and a few years later, because they had become an item, comfortable with each other, they had married.

David put his hand over Joanna's as they sat drinking espressos.

'Wonderful memories! Please try and forget that mad year. I was a fool.'

'I cannot, I feel the wound opening up again. What do you want?' Joanna withdrew her hand.

'I want you back.'

'And you think that you can pop up after thirty years and claim me? Your audacity is quite outstanding.' Her voice was excited and her eyes lit up with delight and anger.

'I'm married and do not intend to disrupt my life again by getting entangled with you. Sorry David, but I'm content with Tom.'

'Joanna, you don't want 'content'. You need ecstatic happiness and I can give it to you. Darling I have longed for you for years and years.'

'While you were 'experimenting' with John? While you were married to Sarah?'

'Yes. There was something missing. It was you. It was us being together.'

'But you managed to stay away. Do you see John now?'

'Not now. I met him in Mougins a few years ago. We were on a golfing weekend. A corporate 'do'. He's married to a French woman and was planning to retire to Provence.'

'So he was also experimenting, or did he marry to cover up his homosexuality?'

'I don't know what you mean.'

'I thought you married Sarah for the same reason.'

'No, I told you, John was a mistake. A dreadful mistake as it turned out. When we met at the alumni reunions you were so cold I decided that there was no hope of reconciliation. Then you married Tom.'

'You didn't come to the wedding, was that because ....?

'Yes, I decided I had to make a life without you and so I went to work in Europe. Met Sarah who seemed to have the same interests and tried to forget you.'

'Oh my God.' Joanna moaned as she began to realise what she had missed and how different her life could have been. She felt tired and heavy. The bright sparkling Florentine air mocked at her misery.

David looked at his watch and signalled to the waiter.

'Darling, please don't be too sad. We can talk tomorrow and every day after that. We've found each other again and we must never lose contact, ever again.'

As they walked across the Piazza della Signoria, barely looking at the statues, David stopped suddenly, turned and put his arms around Joanna.

'I know. We'll meet here in six months and you can tell me if you will consider coming back to me.'

Joanna looked up at him and smiled but he noticed the sadness in her eyes.

'You may not want to make the journey when you know what my answer will be.'

DUSK IN CORFU

Sheila Lockett

In nightly acrobatic show
a pas-de-trois of silent bats
is weaving through the palm tree fronds.
We walk the path down to the beach
as glittering fireflies light our way
and swallows' liquid chittering trill
pours down from high suspended wires.
Soft susurrant waves lap at our feet
their hues of turquoise, gold and red
mirror the colour of the sky.
The sun's vermilion splendour fades;
sinking swiftly through the sea
it pulls the nets of darkness down.
Then lights come on around the bay
bright echoes of the distant stars
we turn and leave the cooling sand.

FOGBOUND

S.E. Ingram

Sounds drift out from swirling fog, goat-like bleating of the shore-sheep grazing amongst the rocks beyond the sea-wall, rhythmic swooshing of waves on the pebbles, high pitched cries of the kittiwakes. I am home. I know every inch of this island, even in this thickest of haas, even though it has been so long since I left. Momentary relief is replaced with constricting panic though, as I see my boy unconscious at my feet, where he slipped on the unfamiliar seaweed, his black city shoes polished and ungripping now dipping toes in the incoming tide, the salt water already staining them. A trickle of blood at his temple is echoed by the polished scarlet varnish of my manicured toes as I look down, the tendrils of fog spiralling around my peripheral vision. I instinctively look with a mother's eye for the rise and fall of his ribcage, as I did when he was a babe in the cot. He breathes. My boy, now a big strong man, impossible for me to move.

Darkness will soon draw in. October brings in winter up here faster than down south, no trees to hold autumn colours, the strong gales sculpting any plant life into stooped horizontal forms, except for the most sheltered spots. This most northerly of the islands, mostly low lying and flat, being the most extreme example. My old family croft Breckfin, is not far though, up the rough track between the fields, the front door sheltered away from prevailing winds. I know Lizzy my sister will be there now, ready for us, though we took an earlier flight from Kirkwall, knowing the weather could postpone all travel for hours or even days. My boy, wandering the island road before supper at the Observatory, drawn to the shoreline by the symphony of unfamiliar sounds, tantalizingly un-revealed by the fog. His precious package in his expensive urban shoulder bag, now lying bashed on the glistening rock at his side. I feel the seals watching me as ever before I see them, glimpses of shiny grey-black muzzle above the water in a brief clearing of fog. I jump, startled as always, as an oystercatcher, peep-peep-peeping his call, swooshes past me at head height and vanishes into the wall of fog again. I bend to briefly stroke Will's forehead, then turn and run for the croft.

Soon I am banging on the sturdy wooden door, hoping Lizzy will welcome me and summon Peter, her husband, and Magnus, their son, to help lift Will to safety. It is years since I have seen them all. Madmen or genius they used to say of the folk of this island. I long ago left the shores for school, university, the well paid career. Lizzy, taken by spells of darkness, leaving only for doctors' visits in her youth. We are both a part of this wild place, born at the same hour, raised on the same hearthside tales, yet so different in our twin bodies. Me hungry for learning and the wider world, Lizzy drawing into the escape of the rich folk tales, the tapestry of island mythology, seeming in part to live in a world of her own construct, narrated by voices I never heard. We lost touch but now I needed her.

I focus on the lichen-covered door lintel; I hear her voice singing one of the old Norse songs as she approaches behind the door. It swings open wide and time melts away as we embrace, differences forgotten in the warmth and shelter, a fresh harvest corn-dolly perched on the shelf just beside us. The men are lifting Will from the shore in no time, carefully bearing him up the track past fresh cut corn fields, and I hear a corncrake's rasping rex-rex-rex call at the wild field margin, tattered poppies nodding in the shelter of the island wall as I stand on the doorstep. Bright pink nerines flower in their sheltered pots beside the step, exotically incongruous, their long stems strong and green. He is safe.

Inhaling a deep breath Will could smell the warming peat fire before the headache throbbed him into consciousness. Softly he could hear his mother's singing voice, for a moment a snapshot of childhood bedtime dreams, but words he could not make sense of, joining with another, almost sweeter voice. His fingers felt not cold damp rock at his sides, but soft woollen fleece. It was dark. As his eyes slowly focussed, he could see over a low, reassuringly thick window ledge to a square patch of starry sky. The fog had cleared. Movement, like a glowing curtain of strange cloud lit from the sea, played across the constellations. Mesmerised, it took him a few minutes to recognise the aurora borealis, the northern lights; he'd seen pictures on a website only a few days before. Warm oatmeal soup was offered to his lips on a large wooden spoon which he drank gratefully, soothed, the comfort of his senses lulling him back to sleep.

'They'll be here for the funeral tomorrow then.'

A gentle question, posed as a statement from Morag, the general store assistant near the landing strip. The pilot of the regular eight-seater plane nodded.

'They just got the connecting flight in time from Glasgow, always running late, those big airports.' He smiled.

The fog had rolled in earlier than forecast, he'd made the last flight in, and then grounded the little plane on the island until it cleared. With a small population, everyone knew everybody's business here, especially a big event like birth, marriage or death, and if it would draw in far flung relatives and acquaintances. He'd seen the crescent of the old moon set the previous night from his sheltered allotment near the Cathedral at his home on the mainland, as he harvested his pumpkins for his children's approaching Halloween party. A dark moon tonight would shroud the island further for the city dwelling visitors.

A radio's music cut to the weather forecast, and expectant chatter fell silent as the large group at the dining table listened intently. The island Bird Observatory acted as hotel, meeting point and communication hub, as well as a twitchers' heaven. The inter-island plane service temporarily halted by the fog, the pilot chatted to the young dark haired woman to his left. She had been on his eight-seater flight in that morning with her fiancé, and he hadn't yet returned from his unplanned walk. It was dark now, and fear was taking hold of her thoughts. He couldn't go far, she was reassured by everyone, but she shuddered at the idea of the unfamiliar fields and rocky indented coastline, even with now clearing weather veiled in the darkness of a moonless night.

'Lizzy,' I whisper, 'what shall we do? We can't move him . . .'

My voice trails into uncertainty. I was always the decisive, sensible one, she the intuitive emotional sister. I feel I am on unfamiliar territory, having been so long away. I don't know how things are done now, which islander to ask for help with what task, as if the fabric of my upbringing had shifted out of my grip.

Lizzy smiled. 'Tam of course, His new wife is the island's nurse.'

I feel my heart race briefly, old memories brought to the surface.

'He's still here, just down the road?' I ask a little too keenly.

Her hand took mine gently.

'He knows . . . he knows about Will. It's ok.'

A wide beam of powerful torchlight scanned across the old cornfield. The search party had scoured the island's road and ditches, and every croft alerted. Tam's voice boomed deep through the earpiece of Morag's mobile phone. She shouted to the group.

'Tam's dog has a scent, he's bolted to Breckfin, might just be the seals hauled up on shore are distracting him.'

They find him there, the dark haired girl's fiancé, warm and soothed somehow, lying on the old sofa in the cold silent croft, soon roused to consciousness. Tam steps over the broken roof slab lying by the front path, where it had fallen as old Peter had a heart attack on the roof, as he checked it ready for the winter. He'd been found the previous week lying there, amidst broken stems of the pink nerines crushed by his fall.

Tam walks to the side of the low roofed croft, looks down the old track to the shore, catching glimpses of dark seals' heads bobbing in the still water, looking back at him. He thinks of the family that grew up here, so near to his; the beautiful twin girls the older islanders joked were descended from the selkie-folk, the mermaids. He remembered the twin with the faraway look, the one who married young in disgrace, already pregnant. She said only that the father was from the sea and sung to her on dark nights. Peter had stepped forward and married her over thirty years ago, their union cut so short by her death in childbirth, the son stillborn. Peter had stayed, helped with the croft, outlived the twins' parents. The other twin, his own love, moved away, drawn by learning and a career that could never be on the island. She had come back, just once, just long enough, and he never heard from her again, or knew of his son, Will, until the reading of Peter's last testament.

The son shone brightly, low in the midday sky, for Peter's funeral. The church was full, all the islanders and Will, in his good black shoes, still bearing salt-water tide marks, with his dark haired fiancée holding his hand tight with relief. As they entered the churchyard they passed rows of lichen covered gravestones. Will stopped at the third as recognition dawned.

Elizabeth Fin, aged 19, died tragically in childbirth. Magnus, son, stillborn.

Other familiar names inscribed above, the family gravestone, marking the plot he had planned visiting with his precious package he had carried with him on the flights. The package of his birth mother's ashes he'd collected from the undertakers, she several years dead, his adoptive family of his twenty-five years still unaware of his journey north.

I had waited so long for him to find me. It's in his blood, this place. I wanted him to find life here, not just death. I think that's what the selkie-folk thought too, those myth woven creatures of the ever present sea. That, I think, is why the seal pup lay on that shore that evening, calling like a mermaid, drawing him nearer, then rearing up and tripping him by the rocks. In life there is death, and in death there is life. And so my son was introduced to the island home he had never known.

HIDDEN SECRETS

Muir Sperrings

Loosely needle stitched in lace
the moss veined leaf is full of grace
It rises from behind a crown
in embroidered threads of gold and brown.

The lustrous petals are a crimson brocade
from vintage ball gowns kept in the shade.
A long, bound stem rises up from the soil
of sap green florist's wire, wound in a coil.

The flower is hung on linen folds
as if dark secrets it withholds.
What if I were to loosen all
and let it fall from plastered wall?

SHADOWS IN GREY

Muir Sperrings

A heavy mist shrouds ancient forms
of granite rocks encased in moss,
While lichen hangs in silver threads
from gnarled, and fissured, ghostly limbs.

Twigs, leaves, and acorn caps abound
upon the decomposing woodland floor.
Nearby, the graceful ferns in disarray
throw phantom shadows on rippling stream.

As the grey shade of day draws on,
the valley shimmers in the failing light.
Stunted and distorted shapes within
engage in dark funereal rites.

16 THE LIMES

Rose Aitken

The place had come on the market six months before the present estate agent had taken it on. The lawyers acting for the elderly woman who had lived there had only just relieved the previous agent of the responsibility of attempting to sell it. It stood large and obtrusive in a built-up area on the edge of a sprawling council estate which had, over the years, encroached upon the once extensive grounds of the place. The old woman had apparently died without making arrangements for the inheritance of the house. There were no living relatives, so nobody claimed it. The money from this sale wouldn't go to the agent who finally sold it. It would go to the government so no big effort had been made by the last agent. As a result, the lawyers had become impatient and changed the seller.

Nobody knew where the name had come from. There were no limes anywhere near the house and, so far as anyone knew, never had been. An old chestnut tree graced the front garden which provided shade. There were some well kept flower beds at the rear of the house and a summer house also. The place looked as if a prosperous family had built it, but now it had rather gone to seed.

It hadn't been added to the estate agent's window yet since there weren't any photographs of it. The advert had been drafted and all the local papers had been told to print at the end of the week.

Damien Walker now walked into the small modern office. His camera hung negligently around his neck. He'd been up at the house taking photos of the place both inside and out. It helped that the garden had been well tended. The tree looked good too; the changing colours of its leaves lending the house a rustic quality which it didn't in fact possess.

Marjorie, his boss, looked up from a stack of cards she'd been sorting at her desk. 'Finished already then?'

To Damien the question seemed superfluous. 'These places don't take long. Do you want to look now or can I have lunch first?' He swung the camera off his neck and dumped it unceremoniously on the desk.

'Have lunch first. By the time you get back this lot should be ready to view.'

The agency had a dark room attached to the premises, but they also had digital cameras for the lesser work. The owner of the small business felt that digital cameras didn't really capture the essence of their more prosperous work. All country houses and cottages got the old fashioned treatment, despite the face that the agency would only get the administration fee, and this included 16 The Limes.

Damien sauntered out of the office leaving Marjorie to move the camera and finish with the index cards. The woman sighed; Damien could really be a handful at times. Still, he did a good job with the houses, she had to admit that. They'd taken him on fresh out of college, where the boy had graduated the previously July with a degree in photography. They intended to train him in the art of public relations and dealing with the media. Damien for his part intended to complete his apprenticeship and move on to something in journalism. The boy had told no-one of this plan, but Marjorie suspected he wouldn't stay long. A certain restlessness, which put her in mind of a cat on hot bricks, accompanied his every move.

No sooner had Damien left the office than Marjorie rose to her feet. Taking the camera off the desk she opened the door of the dark room. For the next hour or so the woman busied herself developing the pictures. They looked good as usual, but something bothered her.

The shop bell tinkled and Damien breezed in through the door of the dark room, not even bothering to find out if light would spoil any developing which might be going on. The boy knew his boss would already have done what needed to be accomplished.

'Come over here. There's something I want to show you.'

Damien obliged at once. 'What is it?'

'Who's that kid in the shot?'

Damien bent over the picture which still hadn't dried properly. It showed the garden taken from the bedroom window. The flowers were mostly dead now this late in the year, but the green of the grass made a vivid splash against the grey sky. A small child, a boy most probably to judge from the short cropped hair and dungarees, stood near the small gate which led into the garden.

Damien scratched the stubble on his chin. 'I don't know. I didn't see anyone there. I suppose he must've wandered in while I took the picture.'

'That's what I thought originally,' Marjorie admitted, 'until I saw this one. He's there again, look, in the doorway.'

Marjorie pointed at the picture. Her brow creased in concentration.

This time she showed him a picture of what appeared to be the living room; though lack of furniture made it difficult to tell since there was more than one room which could pass for a living room. The picture had been taken with the photographer standing with his back to the window, shooting out beyond the door. There stood the same boy. This time they were able to make out the blonde curls and smiling cherubic face. Yet the boy looked strange somehow.

I really don't know.' Damien said. 'I don't remember being disturbed by anyone. In fact, I thought the place looked melancholy. I don't see how we can sell it.'

'Are you sure he didn't wander in and just follow you about?' Marjorie asked. 'He's in all of them.'

'I think I would have known if he'd been there. I'd have heard him.'

'I suppose.' Marjorie's tone didn't sound convincing.

'Can't we use them? A boy in the shot might lend some interest to it.'

'No we can't. I don't want kids in my pictures. In any case it might put prospective buyers off. Vandalism and all that. People are very security conscious these days in case you hadn't noticed. You'll have to go out this afternoon and do them all again and make sure nobody wanders in will you.'

Damien slouched out of the dark room, picking up his camera as he left and checking that it had a fresh roll of film in it. He had hoped to wangle the afternoon off. Not that any real plans had been made, he just fancied some time to himself. Now though, some damn unknown kid had scuppered everything.

Marjorie pondered over the images a little longer then went back to work. There were still things to do before the papers went out for the evening. Her afternoon went fast, making phone calls and rearranging the window displays of photos of houses.

At half past four Damien stomped back into the office, his camera still slung around his neck. 'I've taken all the pictures I can. I've no more film left and nobody came in I can assure you.'

Marjorie looked up at him. 'We'll see about that. Wait here while

I develop them. Better yet, come through and watch the process. You might learn something.'

'I can develop photos you know. I did go to college.' Damien had by now had enough of being patronized by his boss. His temper also hadn't been helped by the fact that he'd forgotten to pick up his wallet that morning so hadn't eaten all day. His mother never let him have a key to their house.

Marjorie shrugged and opened the door to the dark room. By now Phyllis, the secretary, had gone home. Marjorie had told her to; saying that she and Damien would lock up and set the alarm when they left.

Soon they were both busy developing the pictures. Marjorie had resigned herself to the fact that this one would have to go in the Saturday edition of the paper. Still it couldn't be helped. If that kid hadn't been in the shots it would have gone in that night. There would be some explaining to do with the business owner, but Marjorie could cope with that. She'd done it before.

As the pictures cleared they noticed that same boy again. He stood in doorways and at the bottom of the garden. In one shot the child stood erect against the wall. His arms were stretched upwards as though trying to reach something above his head. In another the boy had a small teddy bear which he seemed in the act of tossing from one hand to another. In a third shot the child had tear stains on his face.

'He didn't wander in.' Damien protested before Marjorie could speak. 'I know he didn't.'

'So do I.' Marjorie replied. 'Still it's weird. Didn't you see him when you took the shot?'

Damien gave her a look. 'If I had I'd have told him to get lost wouldn't I?'

'We'll have to get to the bottom of this.' Marjorie turned from the table where the pictures lay drying. She gave him a smile. 'Are you doing anything tonight?'

'I don't think so. Is that an invitation?' Damien grinned.

'It's bloody work, moron. I'm not interested in a date with you; you're not my type at all.'

Damien pretended to look dejected. 'Oh well, what have you got in mind?'

'We're going over there to sort this out.'

'How come you believe me now when I said he didn't wander in?' Damien asked suddenly.

'Because it's the same kid and he doesn't look quite real somehow.' Marjorie sighed and collected her coat from the cloakroom. 'I don't know, just a feeling I suppose.'

They left the office and walked the short distance to number 16, The Limes. It had just started to get dark. The warmth, what little of it there had been in the first place, had gone out of the day. Damien had his camera with him while Marjorie had stopped off at her house to collect a torch. There were no lights in the house, the electricity having been turned off for safety reasons.

They walked up the concrete drive and opened the front door. The house echoed with the sound of their feet on the wooden floorboards. Not a stick of furniture had been left there, not even so much as a chair.

'We should have brought some food with us,' Damien commented. 'I'm hungry.'

'We won't stay long. Then I'll buy you a bag of chips or something.'

'I thought you said it wasn't a date.'

Marjorie punched her companion playfully in the ribs. 'If it were a date little man, I'd expect oysters and champagne, not chips and Coca Cola thank you very much.'

'How do you know I can't supply that?'

Marjorie grinned in the dark. 'Because you work with me, that's why.'

They walked upstairs to the bedroom. Damien stood in the wide window frame, his camera pointing out towards the now dark garden.

'This is where I took the first shot. You can't see much in this light.'

Marjorie took the camera from him and looked through the aperture. She could see the garden but nothing else. 'Have you got that digital camera with you? You know the one you borrowed without my permission last week? The one you haven't returned yet.'

Damien rummaged in his bag. 'Here it is, it should work, I charged it up last night.'

Marjorie took it from him and pointed it at the garden. Still she could only see the dim outline of the flowers or what remained of them. The flash went off, dazzling them, for they had not yet turned on the torch. Now they did so and looked at the picture.

There, just behind the gate, stood the shadowy figure of the boy, his hands covering his face as though he were trying to hide from something. At his feet lay a ball which they assumed he had been playing with. The sky above him looked bright yet outside all light had now gone from the day.

'That is too weird,' breathed Marjorie.

'I told you he hadn't come in. If you ask me he's not real.'

'A ghost you mean? I didn't think boys of your age believed in ghosts.'

'I don't. Do you have any other explanation?'

Marjorie had moved away from the window. Now she began tapping walls with her hand.

'What are you looking for?' Damien asked coming over to her side.

'I'm looking for hollow bits or cracks. See if you can find a seam or something.'

For the next few minutes they both tapped and felt around the walls, going all over the house. Then Damien tapped a section of wall on the stairs which sounded different.

'Is this what we're looking for?' He called out to Marjorie.

She came back upstairs and peered at the wall. 'It could be.'

The house felt cold due to the lack of heating, the gas had also been switched off. Now a tremendous wind blew through the place. Upstairs a window banged, downstairs the front door rattled as the wind gusted. Beside them appeared the figure of the child, he was making a wailing sound. They clung to the banister to prevent themselves from being blown downstairs; Marjorie almost dropped the torch.

Damien felt around carefully with his fingers; at last a portion of the wall moved. With a little more effort he exposed a cavity behind the wall. Marjorie directed the torch beam inside. Damien looked in and nearly lost his balance as the shock of what he saw hit him.

'Jesus Christ', he muttered under his breath. 'It's a bloody skeleton.'

Inside the cavity were the bony remains of a small child. The flesh had totally gone leaving only the whiteness of the bones; they seemed to be intact. Neither of them wanted to touch the remains.

Without thinking, Damien took out his mobile phone and called the police. Marjorie walked slowly downstairs. They could still hear the wailing and crying sound. The wind dropped.

After what seemed too long a time the police car arrived. The bones were taken away from the house for investigation and the two workers went home. Now a story could be attached to it, the place would surely sell. A haunted house with a skeleton to boot. Yet neither Marjorie nor Damien felt inclined to make too much of it. It didn't feel right somehow to mock the dead.

LADY JANE GREY –

The nine days Queen. (1537-1554)

Eva Ziebicki

Hovering over the rocky parkland
Looking out towards the City from Old John
Wind sweeps through auburn hair
Grey-blue eyes
Milk white face
Red-rose lips and gasps
Rustling with nature's sounds
Descending towards the ruins where
The County- known, grand old Tudor house once stood
And home to short-lived childhood years
To marry at sixteen
Made to be Queen by power-hungry mouths
To rule the land
Hailed in the name of religion,

The right way to think
The right way to see...
The soul way
Protestant,
Catholic,
Mutual loathing...

Tonight the ghostly shadow floats across the bracken, cold underfoot
Drifts to the ruins
Where home once stood

WESTENDERS

Roy Iliffe

Michael Davis, in his mid-thirties, lived in an old terraced house in Roman street, off the Narborough Road in the West End of Leicester. He'd been on the dole for years and his main interests in life were eating pizza and watching the X factor; a lazy, sedentary existence which led to a significant weight increase and friends playfully called him 'fat arse, Mick.' Yet Mick or 'fat arse' took it all in good sport.

Anyway, his dynamic wife, Judith, had more than enough energy for both of them. Judith Davis, thirty two, horse-faced social worker extraordinaire was a more formidable piece of work with her devout political correctness, desperate caseload and uncontrollable urge to plaster the windows with Gay Pride, Green Party and CND stickers. But, any differences didn't really matter because they got on so well. They were as comfortable with each other as putting on an old pair of slippers. Sex was still exciting – Judith loved to bite Mick's rolls of fat with her strong, equine teeth. No, a raised voice, cross word or irritated gesture hardly ever passed between them. Until, one evening in November after a day rather out of the ordinary…

It was 7.30pm and Mick was eating a pepperoni pizza, drinking tea and contemplating X factor news and gossip on the ITV website. The central heating and gas fire were on so he was nice and warm, as snug as a proverbial bug. In fact, so engrossed online it was a complete surprise when he swivelled in his chair to be confronted by his dear wife. Judith's face was blue with cold, gaunt and expressionless apart from a brutally stitched on scowl. She wore a muddy red anorak, black bobble hat, jeans and hiking boots and stood aggressively immobile with hands on hips and legs apart.

They stared at each other, uncomprehendingly; a battle of will-power in a pinteresque pause until one of them inevitably cracked.

"You gave me quite a shock," said Mick.

He rammed another slice of pizza into his mouth and chewed and chewed. He laughed, nervously, but it failed to lighten the mood.

"I'm on X factor watch… Simon's in trouble for taking it back to the public vote and not getting rid of Jedward when he had the chance. Jesus! After everything he said about them. It's obvious, they've been headline news and he's worried about the show's ratings."

"Is that all you care about?"

She was patently in a bad mood. Mick feigned indifference by shaking his head and devouring another slice of pizza.

"That and stuffing your face!"

This was an unfair accusation and Mick wanted to put the record straight. He considered, in reply to his wife, that there should be a discernable note of protest but, unfortunately, his mouth was full and when he managed to speak the words came out in a pathetic, high-pitched whine like a squeaky wardrobe door.

"No, no, not at all. This is my tea, Judith."

Her upper lip twisted into a contemptuous sneer as she continued to stare… A medusa stare which went on and on and on. His wife could represent Great Britain if staring ever became an Olympic sport. Mick snapped out of his facile reverie when, in horror comic style, her body convulsed and eyeballs bulged as if about to explode.

"Is… Is there something wrong?"

"Something wrong?" she squealed.

"Yes." Mick shrugged. "I just wondered if something has happened,

today, which has.."

"What?"

"Well, upset you."

"I've been on the bridge!"

"What bridge?"

Judith's body shook and mouth contorted Munchishly as she screamed her feminist head off. Not an ordinary scream emanating from a mere mortal… No, more like a demonic soundscape combining the wail of an air-raid siren with primitive howling from the pit of her stomach. Window panes rattled, pets for miles around dived for cover and neighbours alerted the Noise Abatement Society.

Mick sat with a frown screwed onto his face, utterly bewildered. He'd obviously thrown a piranha into the goldfish bowl… Then it dawned upon him; yes, it all came back in a heart stopping, gut wrenching, visceral flash. The two year campaign that Judith had been involved in to save the historic Bowstring bridge on Western Boulevard from being demolished to make way for De Montfort University's post-modern swimming pool. Judith's Guinness Book of Record's breaking scream gradually subsided until, helplessly, desperately, she ran out of breath.

"Oh, yeah," said Mick. "The bridge."

"You don't understand! When I say I've been on the bridge I don't mean…" She shook her fists. "No, I was chained to it for twelve hours. Yes, twelve hours in the freezing cold!"

"Yeah, it has been…"

"Not just that!" she interrupted. "The abuse I had to put up with was disgusting!"

"Abuse?"

"Yes."

"Who from?"

"The construction workers, you fat bastard! I was preventing them from dismantling the bridge and they hurled the most filthy, obscene, despicable…I.. I can't repeat it. They should respect me. I'm a woman."

"I know you are," confirmed Mick.

"Big, hairy, vile men in yellow jackets and hard hats reeking of sweat, mud and beer. Thick, ignorant Neanderthals with knuckles brushing the ground."

"Well, I doubt if any of them have read Proust."

"Proust? What? What the hell's Proust got to do with it? Jesus Christ, first it's the X factor then it's flaming Proust!"

The unstoppable Judith onslaught machine temporarily ground to a halt in exasperation.

"I'm trying to make a point, Judith, but I can't get a word in edgeways. You care about…"

"There are only three Bowstring bridges in the whole of Europe and when this one's been knocked down there'll only be two."

"Yes," Mick nodded. "I can count."

He raised his eyes to the ceiling and shook his head in despair. This was like a red rag to his militant cow wife who suddenly thrust two fingers in his face,

"Only two left!"

Mick stood up and yanked her hand away but she grasped his other hand and they swayed and lurched in fixed, locked opposition. He knew the depth of Judith's intransigence and that any conciliatory move would, inevitably, have to come from him. Therefore, Mick escaped from her clutches to ride his latest hobbyhorse, viz;- the necessity of a moral dimension in a corrupt show-business world. Unfortunately, he fell at the first fence of the dog-snarling look of hatred on his wife's face and deteriorated into tongue-tied confusion.

"Look, Judith. I know you feel strongly about the.. but there are other..Yeah, like Simon Cowell, the ugly face of capitalism. But.. but the masses..the viewers are fooled by the way he speaks. His oratory, y'know, like Hitler. All mouth and trousers and jokes about his big, high trousers right up… near his chest."

"I don't give a monkey's about Simon Cowell's trousers! I live in the real world chained to a bridge while you sat there on your fat arse! Jesus, no wonder they call you fat arse, Mick!" She pointed at him. "You're really in the doghouse, you are. In the doghouse!"

Mick looked at the woman he married and it all seemed rather absurd. He folded his arms then put a finger and thumb on his chin in mock contemplation.

"Now, where would I rather be? In the doghouse or on a bridge? Let me think…"

THE RIVER

Wendy Edmond

A tunnel of Beech.
Light, and birdsong, filter through
the far canopy.

The lane winds down through
a shifting haze of Bluebells
to where the mill lies.

The deep, dark river
sliding by beneath the wood.
Swans, in the shadows.

A Mallard dabbling
in the slow, reedy shallows
by the stilled iron wheels.

The way to the house
embedded here – ancient stones
and an open door.

Through the wide casement
in the twilight, after rain,
song of the Blackbird.

THE SECRET

C W Greenwood

Angela did not know which way death was coming. Which existentialist had said that everything that had ever happened in life had led to this precise moment? She did not believe it. This moment was due to 'the secret' – the one she had not been able to live with any more. It had seemed safe to tell somehow in this relaxed environment.

The precarious view looking down over the dark cedar valleys below was breathtaking as she stood on the road which was just a narrow ledge winding around the Cyprus mountain. She could hear the car and knew it was coming for her. What would happen then? She had been safe when they thought she did not know. Why had she trusted the man? She had forgotten the rule – 'trust no-one'. But maybe the existentialist – was it Sartre? – had been right and it was her own personality that had led to this moment in time – her own curiosity – her own failure to let things be. Anyone with common sense would have walked away.

Angela remembered how her father had always rebuked her with comments such as, 'Someone with your intelligence should not be so stupid.' Now she was beginning to understand what he had meant and why she had spent her life trying to prove she was not an idiot – only to prove now that she was.

What would Tom do if he were here – if he were still alive? Would he abseil down the mountain? Climb up it? Wait for reinforcements?

All Angela could do was freeze, wait, and listen for the direction. Was the vehicle coming from up the mountain, past her pine forest retreat or from down below winding its way up towards heaven, knocking her down in its tracks? So many questions – why could she not just let things be? And why did it matter which way the car was coming?

Tom had never told Angela the secret but she had worked it out later and understood so many things. She understood why he had been evasive about his timetable and why he had suddenly seemed to have odd impulses such as driving to the Cotswolds to find a particular spot in the woods or deciding to buy a river boat then changing his mind. It was all because of 'the secret'. But did Tom die because of the secret? Even his death was mysterious and not having actually seen him dead she wondered from time to time if he really was. But she had gone to see the death certificate and had been told there was a funeral – albeit a humanist one with few people there. No-one had told her he was dead until two months later. Everything was so weird!

After the other man's reported death (not Tom's) she had scoured the newspapers and did not understand why everyone could not decipher the secret which was so obvious to her now. But 'everyone' had not been recruited and trained by Tom. The newspapers told people what the government wanted them to know. Or even gave them conundrums so that they would jump to the wrong conclusions. In return the newspapers could do what they liked with regard to other stories. That was the deal! The really odd thing was that government ministers were willing to go along with being accused of being responsible for people's deaths when they obviously were not. And yet, paradoxically, knowing this could cause Angela's death. They wanted to keep the secret. They did not want the government bringing down.

Two years after Tom's death Angela had begun to relax and not feel that she might be followed because of her brief association with him, the man she had loved and helped. Initially the attraction had not been his larger than life, slightly manic, character or his warm supportive manner when her father had been dying. No, it had been the enigma. Why had she not taken up Sudoku instead? Tom's sense of humour at times of great pain remained with her.

The sound of the car was still there - approaching and drawing near. Guilt was her other problem. She had been too scared to be with Tom any more and could not cope with being told not to ask questions. He had been taking her life over. She had left him, accusing him of using her. But later she knew he had loved her too, despite his intentions. Why had he died? He had not been ill. Yet apparently he had suddenly developed a heart condition.

Angela had booked in at The Heavenly Retreat in Cyprus on impulse. She and Tom had been there before, three years ago when he had been meeting a colleague in the hills above Limassol. They had enjoyed the walks and searching for wildflowers together. Wild orchids had always been Tom's favourites. Finding a bee orchid, for example, would totally delight him. And Cyprus had so many other species especially in the west or here in the mountains where the moufflon ran wild.

The man at the retreat was friendly, a Scot who lived near Pathos and worked in shipping. He'd come up to the retreat to cool down for a day or two. June this year was hotter than usual down by the coast. He was easy going and had a natural manner when chatting to strangers. She was put at her ease. Of course, ample helpings of the warm sherry-like Cyprus wine helped. He talked about his life and drew Angela into his story then asked her one or two casual questions and she told him the secret. How could that have happened when she had told no-one before? He obviously had a remarkable technique! Then he disappeared. She looked up and he was gone. Assuming he would be back in a moment she waited and waited – not because she wanted his company but because he had the secret. What might he do with it? Eventually she went outside to amble under the pine trees. Tiny fairy lights hung from those nearest to the lodge. The secret would mean nothing to this man would it? He wasn't a journalist or someone who worked for HMG – or was he? How did she know who he was? He could be anyone but surely they were not still watching her all the time and following her around overseas? Were they?

Two totally silent men dressed in black approached her, covered her mouth and escorted her to the back of a van. It had all seemed to happen in an instant whilst the time now had almost ceased to exist. They drove for a while and in the dark Angela could feel the motion of the van going round and round down the mountain road before it stopped and one man said, 'Out!' with a perfect English accent.

So here she was, standing on the mountain road in the dark waiting for death. The car eventually came from below on its way up towards The Heavenly Retreat. The car stopped and she knew exactly who was driving even though she could not see him. The driver was Tom.

Angela's head was full of questions as he opened the passenger door.

CLACKING ORANGE SHOES

Muir Sperrings

The hour is late
windows reflect
dark wind

Outside
Door shudders
it opens
Clacking heels
on concrete
slabs
back
and
forth
Door thuds
it locks

Three minutes
later
?
One clack
and then
Door thuds
it locks

Door shudders
    it opens
    it shuts
    it opens
Another clack
    pause
More clacks
    back
        and
            forth
    back
        and
            forth

Two minutes
    later
Door thuds
    it locks

    silence

BOUNDARIES

Sheila Lockett

I hated the place, always damp and grey. The sodding rain never stopped; days of endless drizzle that didn't seem heavy but soon soaked through your cloak and seeped into your tunic. Colds! I lost count of how many I'd had since being there.

The men were well trained of course and although they grumbled they got on with the job of re-building the wall.

Hadrian ordered this wall to be built to stop any raiding by the northern barbarians. If they wanted to trade, then he would tax them to come through the gates. He needed to stamp his authority on them; and the money was always useful. Unfortunately, over eighty years, the wall had deteriorated a bit. It had been battered and neglected and now leaked barbarians like a sieve.

Well, Severius (our emperor, may the gods bless him) wanted to show his mettle by securing his borders. He originally tried to buy the barbarians off, but that only worked for a while and then they were back to raiding again. That was why we were moved out of our cosy quarters in Chester and shipped up to the cold north. When I say shipped, I mean several days of marching in the wet and murky weather of course; trying to keep the men's spirits up.

Anyway, we ended up at Cilurnum; one of the key forts halfway along the wall. I was made up to quaestor shortly after we got there.

What's a quaestor you ask? It means I look after the pay for the legions in the area, keep the books in order, pay for supplies, that sort of thing. It's a very responsible position. Since being a child I've always had a love for numbers. I have built up a tidy sum playing games with my comrades; not that they like losing, but some men can never resist a gamble.

Promotion meant I moved from the barracks into a house; much cosier than walking the ramparts or mending the defences. It had elegantly painted walls and a mosaic floor in the dining room. I decided to build an underground chamber to keep the money in; better to be safe you know, especially on the border. Had a good strong oak door made for it, iron studded, that would keep thieving hands out.

Soon the fort was getting into proper order, baths re-built and living quarters painted up. Traders were attracted to the legions like fleas to a dog. As more started to set up stalls, so the original small vicus outside the walls expanded.

The sun did shine sometimes, in fact it was shining the day I first saw Erefwen. I wanted a present to send back to my sister who was getting married in Rome. We had a few workmen inside the fort, but I thought something native might amuse her. Musing over some jewellery, I heard the sound of raised voices. Two stalls along the owner was berating this young woman. She was shrinking from his upraised fist and I caught sight of her face turned in my direction. The poor thing looked terrified.

Well, I did what any red-blooded man would do; ambled across and made a pretence of looking at the leather goods on sale. He soon backed off her when he saw me coming. Started fawning over me, being friendly; pointing out the excellence of his wares. The woman had scurried into a room behind the counter. I had at least saved her from that beating. Making a small purchase I returned to the first stall and bought a fine silver necklace which I knew would please Julia.

Throughout the following days the woman's face kept coming into my mind. I would be counting coins and it would appear, making me lose track and have to start again. There was no alternative, I had to return to the stall. She was on her own that day.

"Your husband not here? I was hoping for a word with him."

"No, he is visiting his father, he had word that he is gravely ill."

I looked at her pale face, the shadow of a bruise still visible. Without thinking to watch my words I blurted out.

"Does he hit you often?"

Colour drifted like a rosy veil across her face.

"Sometimes, especially if he has had too much to drink."

I could think of little else to say and left, saying I would return when her husband was there.

I was drawn back the next day. And the next. I couldn't help myself. To me there was an attractive fragile air about her, like a fine drinking glass. She wasn't pretty in the usual way; not earthy and welcoming like many a woman I had tumbled since my youth; nor was she haughty and demanding like the women from my country.

Gradually I got to know her better. Her father was a minor chieftain from the south of the country, he thought her husband was a good catch, having his own business.

On my fifth visit we sat drinking a cup of rough wine. I gazed at the rose tint of her mouth as she continued telling me her story. The air stilled around us as I leaned forward to gently brush my lips against hers. Her dark hair tumbled like clouds around her shoulders. Eyes which I thought were grey now seemed green and fathomless.

Knowing I should get back to my work, I still couldn't resist touching her, my hands clumsy as I caressed her breasts through the soft woollen tunic she wore.

A loud rapping on the shutter brought us back to our senses. Flustered she pushed her hair back from her face and with an apologetic smile she rose.

"I am sorry, I daren't miss any business."

"Of course not, and I should be about mine."

Ducking through the doorway I turned.

"If you would let your husband know, I will call again when he returns. It was good to do business with you."

With those words, I passed the man whose arrival had cut short our pleasant interlude, hoping I had averted any suspicion.

That evening I paid a visit to the brothel. I had to do something; my feelings were getting out of hand.

Lying on the couch under the explicit wall paintings, the face that came to mind was hers, the softness of her lips, the slight scent of her hair as it brushed against my cheek. The girl did her best and I left sated if not satisfied. I paid her well to disguise my lack of involvement.

Why was I obsessed with this woman? Severius was the best leader we had ever had. Under his rule we soldiers were now honestiores - members of the upper class. For the first time we were able to marry during our twenty-five year service. My sister would have found a suitable bride for me. I had all this in my favour, why risk throwing everything away on a native woman.

For two days I distracted myself by working. In the daytime I went to help with the re-building of the wall; stones blistering hands softened by accounting, but I welcomed the pain. It was good to be working alongside the men again. Perhaps it was my isolated occupation that made me dwell on the leather seller's wife.

Her husband returned, of course, in spite of my prayers that he wouldn't. By chance I met Erefwen in the vicus. I watched her tread around a muddy puddle, and saw how stiffly she moved. My arm went out to her as she drew near but she deftly avoided it.

"He has hurt you again."

"He was ill-tempered on his return; his father died."

"You must let me deal with him; I can't bear to see you hurting like this."

"It will do no good, he is my husband."

"Leave him and come with me. I will ask for a transfer, anything."

She looked at me, the pain showing in her eyes.

"How I wish it was that easy. He will never let me go."

With that we parted. I didn't want to bring more trouble on her by keeping her from her work.

The next day I loitered about the workshop until I saw her husband was alone and then approached him.

"I want to put a bit of business your way."

"As you see, my work is of the finest quality. You will be totally satisfied; you have my word on it."

"There is just one thing." I drew nearer and whispered. "I am out to make a bit on the deal for myself. I have been looking for someone I can trust to do business with."

A slow smile crept across his face.

"You can trust me implicitly."

"Look, meet me by the east gate just after sunset. Make sure no-one sees you."

"I'll be there."

My plan was working. I knew he wouldn't be able to resist putting one over on a Roman.

I found him by the gate later and, telling him how to get to my home, asked him to follow me at a safe distance.

"We don't want anyone to see us together do we?"

Arriving at my quarters I poured us both a drink; I certainly needed one. As I discussed my spurious plans with him, I kept re-filling his cup with wine.

"While you're here why don't you come and see my strong room. I am really proud of it; had it built myself."

He followed me down the stairs. Once we were safely inside, I gazed into his face.

"You think you're really tough don't you, beating up your wife?"

He started to bluster.

"She's lazy, just wants to sit about all day. I have to do something to get her to work."

"Well, here's where you get to know exactly what it feels like."

My first blow knocked him back against the wall; he started whimpering straight away, begging me to stop. Her bruised face swam into my thoughts and I kept hitting him.

He lay on the floor, not making a sound and that's when I realised I had gone too far. He was dead. His head was bleeding, he must have caught it on the corner of one of the money chests.

I fetched tools from upstairs and sweated for the next couple of hours, lifting two slabs and digging a hole into which I stuffed his body. He deserved no better.

It was a few weeks before I dared approach Erefwen. I kept my secret from her and no-one ever solved the mystery of her husband's disappearance.

It felt wrong to ask her to live above her husband's grave so I asked to leave the army and persuaded her to come back to Italy with me. While she didn't know her husband's whereabouts she couldn't marry me, but she consented to come with me; at least she felt she would be out of his reach there.

My friends in the legion thought I was mad to retire. As quaestor I could have been considered for a seat in the senate.

I don't regret it. I sit here on my marble bench looking across the straits to the island. The shrill voice of our oldest son breaks into my thoughts. My hand reaches out to caress his sun-warmed curls and the cold, wet feel of the stones on the wall recedes for a moment.

SILENCE IN THE FOREST

Jenny Evans

Watery sun seeping through leaves
highlights the forest floor
Its tentacles spreading ever wider
on the path that goes to war

The early warmth, blanket-like,
wrapping itself around
Murmurings and movement start
Behind the bugle sound

Aching limbs and throbbing heads,
tired from weeks of walking
Stretching, flexing, then man to man,
the muffled sound of talking

Fires are lit and kettles boil
Pots and pans they clatter
The horror of the days ahead
suppressed by mindless chatter

Muskets cleaned, then checked and primed
Boots padded out with hay
Memories of longed for families fade
from the desperate men in grey

Four years of fighting men in blue
In a war that can't be won
So many lost to death and madness
and still it carries on

Later, underneath the trees
Dark clouds have drawn a veil
The silence of the forest haunts
The Civil War Trail

AT THE BLUE HILL INN

Wendy Edmond

The Housatonic River flowed black and fast beside the black wet road. Road and river kept pace with each other while the Jacksons sat up high in the big new rented Chevrolet with the Massachusetts' licence plate, playing Copland and Dvorak's 'New World' on the tape deck accompanied by gusting wind and lashing rain.

On the first day of their trip Stella had hummed 'I took the Chevy to the Levy but the Levy was dry,' but since the blue September skies of New England had succumbed to Hurricane Floyd rampaging its way northwards, she had given up the song. Instead of grounding itself in the Carolinas and dissipating its energy, Floyd had followed the coastline, refuelling from the sea and causing the Jacksons to turn inland.

By mid-afternoon the storm had turned the day dark early. Alex strained to see through the streaming windscreen, the road ahead busy with yellow school buses hurrying to keep ahead of the storm, and men with chain-saws on the wide verges clearing fallen branches they'd pulled from the road.

'If this is only the edge of the storm,' he fretted, 'I'm glad we changed our plans when we did.'

They pulled up behind a school bus disgorging excited children into the drenching rain, sweaters over their heads, clutching each other as they ran for shelter. Alex wound the window down a little and a few heavy drops blew into his face, with a mix of faintly pond-like smells – wet earth and torn grass – blended with the sharp scent of freshly-cut wood. Stella looked up from the map on her knees.

'We turn off soon, first on the left I think.'

A wooden sign above a red mail-box pointed down a narrow track. As Alex turned the car Stella leaned forward.

'Blue Hill Inn! It's down here.'

Alex bumped the big car carefully along the track between dense trees. Stella, looking ahead, saw the narrow wooden bridge first and, beyond it, the house. Beneath the bridge a swollen brown stream rushed headlong into the gathering dark. Alex parked against the steps of the deep shady porch as a man banged open the screen door, head down against the wind and rain, struggling with a large umbrella. He peered through the car window.

'The Jacksons?'

'Sorry – we're later than we thought.'

Alex reached into the back of the car for their overnight bags.

'Not so very late,' the man said, ushering them inside. 'In fact, you did well to get here at all. The traffic reports sounded pretty bad.'

'It was quite exciting.' Stella conceded. Alex pulled a wry face.

'I hope it doesn't get more exciting than that!'

'Theo.' The other man offered his hand to the Jacksons in turn. 'I'm Theo Edson. Welcome to the Blue Hill Inn. Welcome to Vermont.'

He turned and gestured around him.

'Make yourselves right at home. I'll show you your rooms and you can take your time – then come join us. Relax with a drink by the fire.'

Picking up the two holdalls Theo Edson led the way up stairs lined with tightly packed bookshelves and piles of National Geographic and New Yorker magazines.

The Jacksons followed him along the nearest of three corridors leading from a square landing. Their room was large with windows on two sides. A four-poster bed was set between two narrow windows looking out over the front porch and the brown torrent beneath the trees. Opposite the bed a fire flickered in the dark afternoon; a high-backed, winged armchair on each side of it. A small table stood between the chairs holding a decanter and two glasses on a tray.

'I'll leave you to freshen up.' Theo paused by the door. 'By the way – there are no keys to any of the doors; we want you to feel at home. You can drop the latch if you want to, when you retire. Come join us when you're ready.'

Alex pushed up the sash and peered out from the side window. He breathed deeply the scent of the wet grass in small clearings edged with ferns and mossy stones, lying between the house and the thickly wooded slopes, the treetops disappearing into low cloud. The only sounds were of fast-flowing water, wind in the branches, and rain drumming on the roof of the verandah below.

Stella examined the fire.

'It's not real – one of the gas flame things – but cosy, nice.' She turned to Alex, 'I wonder why Theo didn't switch on any lights? I suppose we can?'

Alex turned a lamp on, and off again.

'The firelight is nice,' he said, 'and it's not quite dark outside. Do you think there are bears in those woods?'

Stella looked out at the dripping trees.

'Ask Theo. Probably. I'm going to have a quick shower and change – I want to have a look around downstairs before dinner, it's such a pretty old house.'

Later, as they made their way downstairs again, Alex said,

'Odd – not having a key for the lock.'

'Very.' Stella agreed. 'At least we can drop the latch from the inside, is that the same as locking it?'

In the reception hall a big fireplace housed another glowing gas-flamed fire. A row of wooden decoy ducks stood in line on their single legs along the mantelpiece, and naïve paintings of 18th Century farmyards hung regularly along the walls. More high-backed chairs and a sofa were grouped around an oval braided rug. Unlit oil lamps stood on side-tables, and the recesses beneath the window-seats held more books, half-hidden by heavy plain linen curtains looped back by jute ropes.

Theo stood behind a small corner bar, polishing glasses.

'Great! Come on through and meet Nancy.'

Beside the bar, in a larger room furnished like the first, another grate of tidy flames flickered, flanked by two large dogs, English Mastiffs, who barely managed to lift their heads to look at the newcomers.

'Stella and Alex – Nancy, my wife. Nancy – our guests, Stella and Alex.'

The woman sat in a corner chair, beside an uncurtained window which reflected a lamp set on a low table at her elbow, shedding light across a book on her lap but leaving her face in shadow. She didn't get up, but placed a marker in the page and closed the book, taking off her glasses.

'Welcome,' she said, quietly.

Stella shot a look at Alex which Theo intercepted.

'Sit down, sit down.' He bounded forward and plumped up a cushion. 'What can I get you folks to drink? On the house – a reward for getting here, for finding us!'

'The directions were good,' Stella said.'We had no problem finding you. Alex had the hard job, driving in all that weather.'

Theo handed a glass of red wine to her and a beer to Alex.

'You did well. We're expecting other guests tonight but they've just called to say they'll be late, due to the storm and taking a wrong turning somewhere along the road.'

'And so dinner will be at eight.' Nancy put in.

'Can you wait that long?' Theo seemed concerned, putting on the table in front of the Jacksons a tray with dishes of olives and nuts.

'We usually serve dinner at seven, Chef hates to be late home.'

'Oh – yes, fine.' Alex helped himself. 'You're not too busy mid-week, then?'

'Not right now.' Theo ran his hand over smooth, tanned scalp. 'Mid-September is between seasons – Summer's over and the Fall hasn't gotten under way. It's a good time to come, quiet. We're real busy in the ski season, though – fill all six rooms right through.'

'Have you lived here long?' Alex was curious; somehow the Edsons didn't quite fit in, there was something too – urbane – in Theo's manner.

'Five years this Thanksgiving. We're New Yorkers, both. Nancy taught school. I had a taxi-cab business. We love it here tho' - wouldn't trade places.'

Stella looked about her. 'It's a lovely old house. When was it built?'

Theo looked pleased. 'Late 19th Century, as a hunting lodge. By the time we got to it the estate had been split up but a year back we got to buy the old Guest Cottage and moved our own things in there. Gives another room to let out too. It's about 100 yards behind this house.'

One of the dogs by the fire stretched out and shifted slightly, raising his head, ears pricked.

'Heaven for dogs, I should think,' Stella remarked, 'all these woods.'

'There are bears, though.' Nancy spoke for only the second time. 'We have to be careful. Not let them out to roam at night.'

'Do the bears come up to the house?' Stella tried to sound casual.

Theo's voice was soothing. 'Hardly ever. Maybe in Spring when they're hungry.'

The dogs sat up as a car splashed to a halt in front of the house. Theo went to the door. As her husband returned to the room followed by a man and a woman Nancy stood up. Greeting the newcomers briefly she excused herself, saying.

'Now that you're all here I'll go see how Chef is getting on.'

She left the room, the dogs following, their claws clicking on the polished wooden boards of the floor. Theo drew the guests together.

'Stella and Alex, from England, meet Walt and Zenamara, from Florida.'

'Florida, eh? I bet you wished you'd stayed there, with this weather going on!'

Walt eyed Alex. Tall, thin, patrician, he did not seem to appreciate the comment.

'Yes,' he said flatly, 'right now I do regret leaving Florida.'

The small, dark-haired woman at his side looked quickly up at him and away again, into her glass.

'What an unusual name – Zenamara – where is it from? Did your parents make it up?' Stella was intrigued.

The other woman flushed. 'It is South American. From Brazil.'

Theo glanced from one couple to another. He rubbed his hands together vigorously,

'Ha! Well, here we all are. Sit down, sit down. Get cosy out of the storm.'

Theo busied himself refreshing drinks, producing more nuts and olives. It was completely dark outside now and yet still only one small lamp burned in the big room. Stella shivered slightly. More light, and curtains drawn against the black night, would be cosy. Theo stood quickly as a handbell rang in another room.

'Dinner!' he announced, and led them through the reception hall. The two couples found themselves looking where they stepped, and touching the furniture as they passed. It was difficult to see each other's features in the gloom. Theo showed them to neighbouring tables in front of the window, where flimsy frilled white muslins held back by ribbon bows did nothing to disguise the rain beyond. He lit a candle on each table, and handed out menus before retreating to the shadows at the back of the room to wait. The candle-light, though inadequate, was welcome. The small oval flames danced in the wet, black window-panes and filled the room with shifting shadows.

Alex noticed Walt staring at the menu.

'I cannot even see what's written here!' Alex heard him say, pushing his spectacles up onto his forehead and peering into the edges of the room where Theo waited. 'More light! Can't we have more light?'

'Of course.' Theo moved smoothly forward, switching on lamps.

Walt scowled at the menu. The other three blinked in the extra light.

Stella wished she hadn't left her sweater in their room, it was chilly away from the fires. The menu-cards were for information only as there were no choices in the food offered – Pumpkin Soup; Beef and Cranberry Pot-Roast; Baked Apples with Pecans and Butterscotch sauce.

'All local produce, all in season.' Theo announced as proudly as if he'd grown it himself. A boy and girl who looked like brother and sister served the food at speed and in silence, with many glances at the clock and out of the window. Later, while Theo poured coffee, an old shooting-brake drove past the window and over the bridge. Three heads could be seen inside, lit briefly by the porch lights.

'Our Hansel and Gretel, plus the Chef who doesn't like to be late home,' thought Alex. He was glad the meal was over. Delicious though it had been he had felt uncomfortable in the quiet room, watched by Theo. The cutlery had made a clatter on the plates. Walt had cleared his throat a good many times. Stella had kept up a non-stop commentary on the weather, their day, and the food – the silence had made her nervous and the other couple had resisted all efforts at conversation. Nancy re-appeared to suggest that they take the coffee to more comfortable chairs and led the way back to the hall, the two Mastiffs following her to lay across the front doorway. Theo went to the bar.

'Brandy – on the house,' he offered.

It was more pleasant by the fire. The flames and a black iron bracket of candles provided the only light.The brandy induced a warmth in which even Walt seemed to relax. An amiable mood was sustained through a second pot of coffee and another brandy each. Theo returned to the kitchen with a laden tray, re-appearing almost at once.

'We've got a power outage!' He announced.

Walt stiffened immediately, Zenamara put down her glass with a worried glance at him.

'A what?' asked Alex.

'A power outage,' repeated Theo,'a power cut!'

Stella looked relieved.

'Is that all?' she said, and was surprised to find the Americans staring at her.

'Well,' she went on defensively, 'we've had a delicious dinner. We can sit by the fire in this pretty candle-light and just go to bed when we're ready.'

'It's not so simple as all that.' Theo started to explain. 'It's not just lighting, it's our water supplies too. Every drop we use is pumped up, by electricity, from our own well. No power, no water.'

Stella was undaunted.

'We often have power cuts at home. One clap of thunder and our lights go out. We can clean our teeth in gin!' She laughed, but stopped when she saw Walt staring at her, his mouth set, a muscle twitching at the corner of his compressed lips.

'No water?' Walt spoke to Theo, his voice quiet. 'You say you got no water?'

Theo shook his head. Walt turned to his wife.

'Zenamara – we're outta here!'

Everyone spoke at once. Hadn't Walt noticed it was blowing a gale outside? It was after 10 o'clock – where would they go? All the other hotels for twenty miles around had power outages too, Theo had rung them to check. There was a standby generator, Theo would get it going, Nancy would make hot chocolate on the gas hob. Had Walt forgotten the bears?

Nancy went to the kitchen and Theo, wearing heavy oilskins and with the dogs at his side, disappeared through a back door towards the standby generator.

The four guests were left alone. Alex sipped his brandy thoughtfully. Walt drained his. Zenamara stared into the fire. Stella, to break the silence, said 'Well, we're marooned but safe, dry and well-fed. Let's take it in turns to tell ghost stories!'

No-one answered her. Stella was not put off.

'Cards, then. Let's play cards!'

Nancy appeared with mugs of chocolate and Stella looked around.

'Why don't we just go outside and fill buckets from the stream? Why is no water or light such a disaster?'

Before Nancy could reply Walt spoke, slowly and carefully.

'No power, no water. No water – no showers; no bathing; no flushing.'

Stella tried to placate him.

'Theo's probably got bottled water if you want to drink it. There's bound to be enough in the hot-water tank to wash your face, and filling buckets from the stream is the answer to flushing!'

Walt stared at her. He said quietly,

'You don't understand. It must be different in England.'

'No Dunkirk Spirit, sweetheart.' Alex murmured between sips of hot chocolate. 'You're not getting through …'

Theo and the dogs re-appeared, water pooling beneath their feet. 'The standby generator can't cope. I'll try to get a replacement come morning. I'm sorry, folks.'

Walt stood up. 'We can't stay. C'mon, Zenamara, we're leaving.'

'Everyone around here's closed. No power.' Theo shrugged.

'We'll just drive.'

'But it's wild out there!' Alex was shocked. 'There'll be fallen trees on the road, the rivers are up – '

Stella looked at Zenamara.'Where will you go?'

Zenamara raised her hands palms upwards as Walt came down the stairs with their bags.

'I booked four nights,' he said to Theo, 'I need a refund.'

'I can't refund your credit card without power.' Theo replied. 'You're gonna have to trust me.'

'I'll take cash, or a check.'

Theo shook his head.

'Refunds have to be made in kind.' Theo refused to give in to Walt's increasingly annoyed insistence that his money be refunded there and then, and at last Walt turned and, followed by Zenamara, left the house. The screen door banged shut behind them.

No-one spoke as the sound of the car engine died away. Nancy stood up.

'When you've finished your chocolate Theo will show you the night arrangements.'

'Night arrangements?' Alex queried, doubtfully.

'Follow me.' Theo rose to his feet and led the way behind the bar. In a long corridor he placed a battery powered lamp beside a telephone.

'This is the house-telephone,' he explained. 'If you need assistance in the night just pick up this and it will ring beside our bed.' He pointed to a door at the end of the corridor. 'Through that door is a path to the

Guest Cottage, where we'll be. If you need to, you get out through that door. It's never locked. There is no lock.'

'What else is along here?' Stella was curious.

'Just the laundry, and the drying-room where guests dry their boots and so on in the ski season.' Theo told her.

'Are you saying that we're here on our own?' Alex was disbelieving.

'Oh, we never stay in the house. Make yourselves right at home. We're just a 'phone call away. Breakfast is at eight.'

He turned back towards the door, and gave the Jacksons a battery-lantern each.

'Sleep well.'

Before they reached their room the Jacksons heard the distant bang of the outer door at the end of the corridor. Stella picked up some back numbers of the New Yorker and the National Geographic from a stack near the top of the stairs. Once inside their room Alex dropped the latch.

'Right,' he said purposefully. 'If we need to, we can get out to the car through the front windows. Slide down the porch roof. The sashes run easily, I tried them earlier.'

Stella looked up from one of the winged chairs beside the fire, where she had settled with the magazines.

'What are you talking about?'

'We have to have a contingency plan.' Alex was dragging the other armchair to the door as he spoke. 'Good. These are quite heavy. I'll need that one, too.'

Stella watched as Alex tipped the chair at an angle and jammed it between the walls in the narrow hallway before the door.

'You can sit on the bed.'

The second chair he arranged facing in the opposite direction to the first, bracing it firmly in place.

'We should sleep in our clothes. Leave your shoes by the window.'

'Just what are you expecting to happen?'

'Anything. I don't know. None of this feels right to me. Does it to you?'

'How do you mean?' Stella sat crossly on the bed against the pillows.

'Think about it.' Alex perched beside her. 'They're a pretty odd couple, you must admit. Everywhere else we've stayed the hosts have been busy, not reading books in corners, in the half-dark. They don't seem naturals at the job.'

'We-ell.' Stella mused, but Alex went on, 'and the dogs, they weren't natural either. Took no notice of anyone. And why doesn't the Chef like to stay late? And those two who served us at dinner – they couldn't wait to get away. Why no keys to the doors? This place is open house to any weirdo who cares to come in. There isn't even a bloody 'phone in our room!'

'There's one in that corridor.' Stella reminded him.

'If you think I'm leaving this room to go to a distant 'phone that only connects to their place then you must be joking!'

'There must be a proper 'phone. Theo called the other hotels in the area to check on the power situation.' Stella remembered.

'So he said. How do we know he did? I didn't see or hear him, did you? And what about that other couple? What was normal about them taking off in this weather at 10 o'clock at night in the pitch dark?'

'So what exactly have you barricaded the door against, Alex? And you're going to have to move one of those chairs soon because you've blocked the bathroom door.' Stella added.

'How do you know that Walt and What-ever-her-name-is have gone away? They might be in it with Theo and Nancy, and are with them right now, waiting.' Alex lifted a curtain and squinted at the stormy blackness beyond.

'Waiting for what?'

'For us to go to sleep.'

'And then what?'

'They'll come and get us. The kitchen must be full of carving knives and meat cleavers.'

Stella looked at her husband for a long moment before turning back to her magazines.

'You've been watching too many old Hitchcock movies,' she said, 'they've given you ideas.'

'The chairs and the door will hold them for long enough for us to be out of the windows and down the porch roof. Leave the bags, packed, under the windows. I've got the car keys in my pocket.'

Stella sighed and put down her magazine.

'Actually, Alex, there is something else that worries me more.'

'What?'

'Bears. Vermont is full of bears. They're very big, and very strong. They can rip locked car doors off, and their claws are six inches long. You've heard that story about the guy walking in the woods who asked a Ranger how to tell the difference between a Grizzly and a Brown Bear?' Stella went on, 'well, he told him that the Grizzly will climb a tree after you, and the Brown Bear will shake it until you fall out. Or was it the other way around? And now,' Stella went on, 'I really need to get into the bathroom.'

* * * *

Deep into the night Stella dreamed of a large, dark bear shape padding silently out of the woods, through the back door and along the corridor, and up the stairs. Pausing on the landing to sniff the air, its great head swayed from side to side, jaws slavering, as it turned along the corridor towards their room, filling the narrow space with its massive bulk. As the dream bear pushed against the door of their room she woke, the flickering fire giving enough light to show her Alex's face as he muttered and fidgeted in his sleep.

* * * *

The sound of a car engine woke them. Opening the curtains Alex saw the reluctant kitchen staff enter the house by a side door. The morning light was pale and grey and the wind had dropped. It had stopped raining. Alex looked at his watch.

'Seven. Breakfast in one hour. I thought that was a tad early when Theo told us last night, but now I can't wait to get on our way.'

He dragged the two arm chairs back to their places either side of the fireplace and began to change his clothes.

'We made it, then?' Stella remarked.

'So far, so good.' Alex grinned.

The welcome smell of coffee hung in the air as Stella and Alex reached the hall. The dogs looked up from the fireside and wagged their tails. Theo was arranging copies of 'The Boston Globe' on the bar counter. He smiled.

'Good morning! Sleep well? Ready for breakfast?'

Theo led them to the dining-room and Alex glanced through the screen door. The Chevy was still there, beyond the porch.

As the Jacksons took their places at the table thin sunlight broke through the high cloud. Nancy brought a jug of aromatic, steaming coffee and Theo offered to take their breakfast order.

Alex looked curiously at their hosts' faces. Theo smiled at him, meeting his eyes. Sounds of banter came from the kitchen and, as Nancy swung back through the door, of someone laughing over the sharpening of knives.

POOR BURU

Eva Ziebicki

(The night we said goodbye to our dear old cat)

Feeling numb,

She's crying out loud.
Helplessness limply begging for a remedy

Speaking to me, blind with pain
I feel her tummy

Stabbing like ten knives,
As her wilting body recoils into the wall,

Forced into a corner

I see her there
Eyes accept the warmth of my hand

Holding the limp body like a rag doll, wet,
head drops.

Placed her in the box,
she releases her call,

Crooked and bent
A wail and she stops.

No sound
No scratching
No tearing down the walls to freedom

We arrive at the clinic
We watch
Where she lay on the table

Good bye Buru,

Sweet thing.

SAY IT WITH FLOWERS

Ann Fuchs

'Pink and white would be excellent.'

James Maxwell looks across the shop, narrows his eyes, and smoothes his greying hair, as he listens to the person on the other end of the line.

'I can make a nice dainty arrangement. I have just the flowers in mind,' he smiles down the phone.

'Could you let me have the name and address?' He writes down the details.

'Oh, is that Sadie Macdonald's mother? I didn't know she'd gone into the Murrayfield Home. Och, she's such a lovely lady.' He looks around. The shop is empty. He can hear his wife chatting with the trainee in the back as they assemble the tributes for the day.

He lowers his voice.

'So you're her niece. Which side of the family do you come from?'

A pause and he nods his head solemnly.

'But of course, the Cameron family are so well known in Edinburgh. And you're a long way from Sadie. Leicester is it?'

'James,' his wife enters noiselessly, which was unusual as her high heeled boots normally made a tapping sound on the wooden floor. He quickly changes his voice from that of confidante to one of a salesman.

'Well, Mrs. Brassington, I have your details and that will be £40.00 including delivery. I'll make sure that it's delivered on the morning of the tenth. Thank you so much for your custom. Maybe we will speak again. Goodbye.'

'Who was that you were talking to? What about the Camerons?'

'Well, dear, you remember Sadie MacDonald?'

'Rather difficult to forget after what happened.'

'Well, her dear mother, Mrs. Cameron, is now resident in the Murrayfield. Probably on level three and we all know what that means.'

'James, don't start. You have got yourself into trouble before. Just button it.'

Mary then goes to one of the many large zinc vases, picks out long stemmed white lilies and takes them out to the back.

James looks across from the counter and not for the first time admires his shop. It is classy and modern. Not like the frippery shops near the station where they sell mixed bunches of flowers. The blooms, each colour and kind in their own container, are large and luxurious. Their scent reminds customers that they have to pay the price for quality. He opens the door and walks outside into the sun to look at the display along the green painted front. The bay trees either side of the door are trim like sentinels on guard.

'Hello, Mr. Maxwell, and how are you today?'

'Ah Mrs. Buchanan, blooming, naturally, but how is your daughter now?'

'I haven't seen her for a few days, but she does work so hard. She has such a demanding job at the gallery. Have you seen her latest exhibition?'

'But, I thought she had been a little under the weather. We sent her a lovely arrangement, just right for her ….' James's voice trails into silence as he looks at the old lady's horrified face.

'Mr. Maxwell what are you talking about? Janice rang me just two days ago and she didn't mention she was unwell. You must be mistaken.'

'Yes, yes, of course. Uh, ah, it wasn't Janice Buchanan. Um, if I remember correctly, it was a Janet Buchan. Silly me. I am sorry to upset you, dear Mrs. Buchanan. Let me make amends and give you a little nosegay.' James rushes into the shop, covering his embarrassment with action, picks out a tiny bunch of violets and hands them to the old lady outside the door. Mrs. Buchanan, still looking shocked, accepts them cordially.

'There's no need, but they are lovely. Thank you, Mr. Maxwell. Well, I must be going about my messages. I think I'll ring my daughter and see how she is.' She laughs nervously. So does James.

Mary, elegant in black trousers and jacket, looks sternly at James as he enters the shop.

'And how is Mrs. Buchanan? I hope you didn't say anything about Janice. We do have to be discreet in our profession. People may tell us all sorts of gossip but it mustn't go any further. Sadie Macdonald is a lesson to us all.'

'Now, Mary, don't go on. I'm a reformed man.' Putting his arm around her shoulders, 'But, my dear, you're not perfect.'

'Yes, I admit that. We lost some good business and that certainly taught me to keep my mouth shut.'

Mary turns, kisses him on the lips and walks towards the back.

'Did she pay for them?'

'Pay for what?'

'The violets, dear.'

'Oh yes.' James reaches into the pocket of his green trousers for the correct money to put into the till. To divert her attention he calls after her.

'Have you put in the order for the red roses? We only have ten days until Valentine's Day and you know our customers like to buy in dozens.'

'Yes, I've upped the order by forty eight stems.'

James relaxes and laughs. 'Oh my dear do you remember Mr. Leslie buying two dozen and wanting them wrapped separately. I had to bite my lip.'

And in a quieter voice, 'What do you think he was up to? All those excuses about ease of carrying. Did he really think we were that naïve?'

'Whatever we think, it doesn't matter but he must feel confident that we'll not spill the beans. Although, it's interesting that Mrs. Leslie never buys her flowers here. He knows his secret's safe.' And laughing and winking. 'What ever it is.'

'Sadie Macdonald is a lesson….. Was Mrs. Buchanan taking those violets to Janice? How is she now?'

James mumbles guiltily 'I don't know how she is or if they were for her. Remember, dear, discretion.'

Mary smiles benignly at James. Their conversation is interrupted by a customer entering the shop.

Later, when they are alone, 'You know, Mary, the Sadie Macdonald fiasco was not a total disaster. She still used us for her wedding flowers. Admittedly she hasn't ordered anything since. But she must be thinking about us again as she recommended her cousin to ring us.'

'True, but, how embarrassing. I mean, she lives below my parents.'

'But we didn't make it up. Wasn't it Lorne who told us? He's normally a reliable source.'

'You're right. Och, I just wanted the ground to open up right there in Heriot Row. Sadie was so nasty. It would've helped if I had not pressed her bell instead of Mother's, but then to make a comment like that about her new husband was unforgivable, unutterably gross.' Mary was beginning to flush with embarrassment again.

'Well dear, you've learnt your lesson. You know what they say. Engage brain before mouth.'

'Cheeky! Pot calling the kettle black?'

She walks towards the back of the shop then turns round.

'I'm sure that Lorne was right.' She whispers. 'Sadie's husband's ex wife did give him a hard time when they divorced. They say he went to her with nothing but the clothes on his back. That Sadie Macdonald protests too much. No doubt she's the one keeping him in Jags and malt.'

Nevertheless, as Mary walks into the back she shivers as she recalls the distress she had caused within the close village community of Edinburgh, with such gratuitous gossip.

THE HARVEST MOON

Muir Sperrings

shines bright
in the September sky;
no passing cloud
to darken the way
of one small wood mouse
whose tiny feet
and tail
curl round
a fragile dried out stalk
She makes as if to leap -
the umbrella full of seeds
above
curves downwards
to the earth
and scatters them
far and wide;
a hungry mouse
gathers all
then hurries back
to her dry burrow
there to store and feast.

THE MIGHTY SCARE

Eva Ziebicki

Long, long ago there lived an old Captain called Bluetoes. He lived onboard an amazing galleon called The Mighty Scare together with his merry crew. Bluetoes' finest mates were old man Barnacle, and Crocker with a long scar on his face. Another mate, Joe, had teeth as yellow as buttercups and grinned all the time. They had all known each other since the early days when they all used to sail in The Mighty Scare to exotic islands in the Pacific, purely to sunbathe and drink fresh coconut juice on the rocks by the seashore. The three men always helped Captain Bluetoes take charge of the ship and its rowdy crew.

Crocker used to sit on a wooden bench at the front end of the galleon and beat his hands slowly on the big, bass drum. The fifty-strong crew pushed and pulled the massive, wooden oars into the ocean waves as they sailed towards a new adventure. Meanwhile, on this particular voyage Captain Bluetoes steered the galleon due north towards Westerly Island, a place where they had so far never been. It was known for its rough seas and jagged rocky coastline. He breathed in the morning air and as usual he brushed loads of shaving foam all over his stubbly face and sang sea shanties as loud as a trumpet. And this he did every morning whether or not it was raining, without fail, as the ship sailed smoothly across the vast ocean.

As usual, Captain Bluetoes issued his orders, "My good man, Barnacle, send the thinnest boys or men up to the crow's nest to make sure there are no sea-monsters heading towards us or worse still steer away from any awful pirate ship with a skull and crossbones on the flag. That would mean real trouble and so far The Mighty Scare has never ever encountered any such problems. Above all, our flag is far scarier than any other pirate ship's flag I am sure of it," said the Captain.

By now the crew was getting hungry, and Captain Bluetoes couldn't wait to eat his dinner. It was Joe, last but not least, who did all the cooking. He provided the fishing tackle for the best fishermen on board the galleon. The food on board ship was absolutely delicious.

"I'll set to work on a scrumptious feast for dinner," said Joe saluting the captain and running down below deck to start cooking the chips.

The galleon itself was over a hundred years old and well used by all accounts. Some of the crew said it was old and rickety. The floor boards creaked even when the skinniest crew members walked across the deck, from port to starboard. The galleon's sails were tattered and torn. In fact, the only decent part of the entire galleon was Captain Bluetoes's bedroom. The bedroom had polished, wooden walls, lots of paintings of his pirate mum and dad, and two small sketches of his pirate girlfriends who have since left the ship for various reasons. Next to his bed Bluetoes had a poor old parrot called Beauty and she woke up Bluetoes every morning at the same time, without fail.

Everything was wonderful, as usual on board The Mighty Scare until all of a sudden something terrible happened.

"I've got to tell you....I keep rowing, Crocker," said one of the oarsman crew- members, "...but the ship doesn't appear to be moving."

Then the captain appeared. "And why isn't The Mighty Scare moving?" he bellowed.

Crocker blushed. He also looked slightly embarrassed that the captain hadn't noticed pools of water beneath their feet, "I think the ship is sinking," said Crocker.

No sooner had Crocker spoken when torrents of rain came pouring down. Water was gradually rushing into the ship. A floor board went gush into his hand. There was chaos on board the galleon. Moreover, several prisoners had managed to escape from below deck.

"Let's search for the treasure chest in the Captain's room," said a boy called Billy.

Captain Bluetoes couldn't stand Billy. He was the leader of all the prisoners. He was fast and sneaky and he was also very clever. What was worse still was that the boy had managed to break in to the weapons cupboard. He stole dozens of swords and the Captain had no idea about it. He was far too busy trying to get all the water out of his bedroom and calm down Beauty the parrot, who was most distressed.

Before the Captain knew it, the entire crew and the prisoners were knee-high in water. A massive fight broke out on deck between the captain's men and all the prisoners on board the ship. Swords clashed and many men and the occasional woman went overboard. Both sides fought hard until they would not stop fighting and glug, the ship began to sink. Slowly, slowly, the galleon sank to the bottom of the ocean.

Only a few of the crew and a dozen or so prisoners survived, or so the story goes.

Some say that they swam to the island that looked far more beautiful than the last one they had moored at... Barnacle, Crocker and Joe, forever faithful, sat next to the captain on the rocks whilst Beauty squawked in her cage beside them.

"At least it's a glorious, sunny day," yawned Captain Bluetoes.

"I can go and find us some coconut juice if you like," said Crocker, spitting out a small fish he thought he'd swallowed.

"Jolly good idea," said Captain Bluetoe lifting his head up towards the sun.

"At least we haven't got to swim in dangerous waters," sighed Joe. "The sea's calmed down now," he said.

"That's true," grinned Barnacle, giving Billy the ex-prisoner a nudge in the ribs.

From that time onwards there was no more fighting between Captain Bluetoes and Billy, or any of the others. They even found a row of caves which they slept inside at night time.

After seventy days, a ship found them and before they knew it, the survivors, Captain Bluetoes, Crocker, Barnacle, Joe including a few more pirates, were all on their way home again, after a rather memorable adventure... just thinking about when they could start their seafaring voyages all over again....

OFF THE TOP OF MY HEAD

Jenny Evans

An office in central London, sometime in the mid 1950's

I have been summoned, and so here I sit in a rather uncomfortable upright chair, awaiting my fate. My hat sits at a jaunty angle in its normal place on the coat stand in the corner. Jane greets me with her usual kiss on the cheek, and after straightening my already straight tie, indicates that I should sit and wait. She is working behind her desk, but every now and then she looks my way and our eyes meet. I see a promise there that may never be fulfilled, only time will tell.

Having recently returned from a rather unproductive trip to South America, and pleased to be back in London on this rather chilly autumn day, I am more than happy to sit with my thoughts and just wait.

"Would you like a cup of tea?" Jane asks, breaking the silence.

"That's kind, thank you."

I watch appreciatively as she walks back and forth across the room, her high heels silent on the faded red carpet. When she hands the steaming drink to me there is a biscuit in the saucer.

"I thought you might like a ginger nut."

"I would, thank you."

As I tell this small untruth, I feel the heat rising in my face.

I actually hate ginger nuts. I have hated them since I lost a tooth whilst biting into one at school, and then crunched the tooth along with the biscuit. But eating one is a small price to pay for Jane thinking about me in a different way to all the others. I am very relieved when she goes back to her typing and I am left to my thoughts.

Lying was never my thing. I was, and continue to be, a pretty hopeless liar. I had it drummed into me from an early age that lying was wrong. If I was caught out telling even just a small fib, my father would take great delight in telling me that all liars go very swiftly to hell and burn in eternal damnation.

Now I'm not saying that I actually believe all that nonsense, but somewhere deeply ingrained within me is a guilty conscience, ready to pop out at the most inconvenient moments.

When I was away at boarding school I developed an almost uncontrollable fascination with gadgets. At night when my contempories were sound asleep, I could be found creeping down to the lab where I would spend many happy hours trying to convert a fountain pen into a rocket launcher, and other undertakings of the same ilk.

Occasionally on the way back to my dorm I would hear the dreaded words,

"Boy. Yes you boy. What are you doing out of bed at this hour?"

My stuttering explanations, which involved nothing of any sense, lead to more than one meeting with the headmaster's cane, and taught me how to be a lot more careful when moving about places where I wasn't supposed to be.

When I left school and entered my chosen profession, it was a prerequisite of the job to be able to lie convincingly. Because of this I learned to prepare for any potential situations in advance and tried not to leave anything unplanned. Mostly this worked well, but on the odd occasion when I had to think of something off the top of my head I would bluster and bluff and hope I sounded convincing. Luckily this didn't happen often and I also learned that charm went a long way, especially with the ladies.

I lost my virginity to a girl named Bubbles Barclay when we were both fourteen, and definitely much too young to know any better. What we lacked in experience, we made up for in enthusiasm, and continued practising until the day her mother discovered us by the rhododendrons and she was sent to stay with her aunt in Cornwall. I still see Bubbles occasionally with her 'oh so proper' husband, and she always greets me with,

"Hello James darling. How are things down south, still looking up I trust," followed by a very exaggerated wink. Quite a girl Bubbles, I shall always be fond of her.

As the years went by quite a number of women crossed my path. They all had three things in common. They were highly intelligent, extraordinarily beautiful, and they all had very unusual names. Blondes, brunettes, redheads, unique in their own way, and we enjoyed each other's company enormously. Unfortunately, for the most part, they proved to be utterly untrustworthy.

These were the people who were the trickiest to lie to. There is something about sexual attraction that bares the soul, and the physical closeness to another human being opens the way to disclosure. Once or twice I probably said more than was wise, and I created problems for myself that, of course, had to be remedied. I was sorry when one of them touched my heart, as I knew what the final outcome would be. I had no choice but to walk a solitary path.

As the years passed, and I progressed ever upwards in the firm, I received the highest accolade that was possible in my profession.

To be able to represent my country in this way was a badge of honour to be worn with pride and total secrecy. I was now back playing with the gadgets I loved so much, travelling the world and so far surviving my escapades.

I notice my tea has gone cold so, along with the half eaten biscuit, I put it down on the table next to me. The intercom buzzes. Jane answers it immediately. A familiar voice speaks.

"Moneypenny, please send Mr Bond in."

As I stand, Jane looks up at me,

"M will see you now 007."

IN THE FOOTSTEPS OF CAESAR

Sheila Lockett

Here in the sacred area,
scene of Caesar's brutal death
confetti cats now roam
in sanctuary.
Sleekly feral cats who sit
as cosy pairings in the sun,
or singly walk with wary eye
and lightly tread the marble blocks
where mighty emperors once stood.

Sharp claws hidden in soft paws
suddenly expose in fight,
yowling echoes of the men
with murderous knives.
The conflict over, peace returns.
While vanquished slink
beneath the stones
to dark and secret hidden niche;
the victors strut and preen
where emperors once stood.

ANOTHER MIRACLE

Roy Iliffe.

It was snowing outside 42 Eastfield Street on Christmas Eve. Snow lay thick on the pavement and flakes gently swirled in the bitter cold. Sheila Porter was in the kitchen of her terraced house removing giblets from a turkey. Her hair was going grey and she wore a pinny from a holiday in the Lake District over her flowery dress. A decent, respectable woman with a middle-aged bulge who suffered more than her fair share of problems and the main one, her daughter, Debbie, was standing right next to her. Debbie was twenty-one and unemployed. Since leaving school she had slobbed around for five years but at the weekends went to night clubs and wild, crazy parties until the early hours of the morning. Her only saving grace was her natural beauty and Sheila could hardly wait for the day when she would settle down and get married. Blessed with raven tresses, cobalt blue eyes, flawless skin and a voluptuous figure there were plenty of male admirers. Yet the only suitable candidate, a Chartered Accountant called Nigel, was unceremoniously dumped in favour of a series of degenerate, hopeless cases with no prospects, whatsoever. Debbie's latest heart-throb played bass guitar in a new age retro glam band. In a generation gap impasse Sheila refused to rise to the bait when his name was casually mentioned. Besides, it was time for a Christmas truce on these heated debates.

"He looks just like Pretty George in 'The Pink Shockers.'"

"Who does?"

"Sam. My boyfriend!?"

Sheila had never heard of Pretty George but she knew Old George.

Yes, Old George was her bald-headed, snub-nosed husband who, at that very moment, was in the bedroom playing with their son's present. Sheila was getting desperate. They were expecting a visit from Arthur's family and she was way behind schedule. Her heart sank at the prospect of their arrival. George was weird but his younger brother, Arthur, took the broken biscuit. God alone knew why she had married into such a peculiar family. Her brother-in-law hardly knew what day it was, his wife, Enid, could nag for England and their son, Wayne, lived in a world of his own.

"There's so much to do. Your Uncle will be here any minute and I've got to lay on a turkey."

"I didn't know there was going to be a cabaret," Debbie replied.

"Oh, that's very funny. You think you're so clever, don't you, with your smart remarks? Well, it's not clever at all. Why can't you just sit on the sofa and quietly watch television like cousin Wayne?"

Debbie shook her head in despair. She was as different as chalk and cheese from a sixteen years old greasy, bespectacled nerd in a beige leather jacket. Wayne was just sad.

"I couldn't be like him."

"No, I know you couldn't. You'd rather go out with all the boys under the sun."

"I'm in love."

"What on earth's been going on?"

Before Debbie could elucidate the doorbell rang. Sheila flew into a panic and yelled upstairs to inform George that his brother had arrived. Arthur's family dressed soberly, drably and were religious in name only. They never went to Church but devoutly watched 'Songs of Praise.' Unfortunately, Arthur wasn't the best company during the festive season because, apart from being crippled with arthritis, he hadn't uttered a word for three years. No, not one; for some strange, inexplicable reason he had clammed up. Sheila helped Arthur manoeuvre into the best armchair in the living room then poured sherry from her silver service trolley into slim, delicate glasses. His wife, Enid, a formidable woman who dressed in black and never stopped complaining, lowered her enormous bulk on to the chair next to him.

"I can't tell you how much I've suffered. How would you like it, eh? Looking after a pathetic, disabled mute twenty-four hours a day. He needs constant attention all of the time. Yes, it never bloody ends!"

Arthur was thin, drawn, gaunt with green, beady eyes and a single strand of brown hair combed over Bobby Charlton style. Oblivious to everybody he raised a quivering hand to thin lips and tried to sip his sherry but ended up dribbling most of it down his cheap Marks and Spencer's suit. Enid tutted, grabbed a sherry and downed it in one... Her mood changed when she saw her niece. Enid beamed with delight, stretched out her flabby arms and enjoyed the traditional Christmas greeting of squashing Debbie's face into the folds of her heaving bosom. As it was a ritual Debbie had grown accustomed to over the years she merely wiped her face on her sleeve and flopped onto the sofa next to cousin Wayne.

Sheila took the opportunity to slip out and, once upstairs, she hammered on the bedroom door.

"Come down, George! Your relatives are here! Why have you locked this damn door?"

George wondered what the commotion was and opened the door

a fraction. Despite Sheila's entreaties he flatly refused to join the others. Infuriated, she stormed back down the stairs but George stopped her in mid-tracks with the strangest of requests; yes, for two pounds of sugar, a roll of electric wiring and a can of weed-killer. Sheila stood at the foot of the stairs, dumbstruck, then her enigmatic husband disappeared from the landing.

Sheila scratched her head in bewilderment but there was no respite in the living room what with Enid, in the process of recounting her troubles, mercilessly pulling Arthur's lack of personality to pieces. A tear ran down the victim's cheek and Sheila, heart full of pity, tenderly dabbed him with a handkerchief. On the sofa Debbie hitched up her black skirt and mischievously sprawled over cousin Wayne who was consulting a magazine balanced on his lap.

"Seven o'clock it's 'Doctor Who.' Eight o'clock, 'Casualty.' 'Nine o'clock News.' At ten past nine it's 'Little Britain.' Then it's 'Bridget Jones' Diary 2' followed by 'Carols from King's College' and a late night horror film."

"Oh, Wayne. I've missed you so much."

"What?"

"I'm crazy about you. Don't you love me, anymore?"

"Get off! I'm watching the telly."

She had never been rebuffed before.

"What have you got between your legs – the 'Radio Times?'"

"Yes," said Wayne.

He took thick, black glasses off and squeezed a spot on the bridge of his nose.

"Ugh, my God! You're disgusting!"

Debbie recoiled in horror in the face of his appalling lack of etiquette but her mother didn't seem the slightest bit interested. Sheila was otherwise engaged explaining to Arthur that his elder brother was doing something very strange in the bedroom. Enid laughed like a demented seal.

"Arthur can't hear you. He's catatonic."

"I didn't realise he was catatonic," Debbie replied. "I just thought he was a bit quiet."

Debbie concluded that they were all a dead loss. Her thoughts turned to an important reason why her parents should like her boyfriend, Sam, indeed, take him into the bosom of the family. The only boyfriend she had ever introduced to them was safe, wet Nigel who they had welcomed like a long lost son. Sam wasn't like Nigel. No way. Whereas, Nigel flew off the scale on the nerdometer Sam was the epitome of trendy cool. When she thought of him it made her knees tremble, gave her goose bumps but still realised he wasn't everyone's cup of tea. She calculated chances of success. Though her mother would detest the radical concept of a young man with a penchant for transvestism she could always rely on her dear, old Dad. Not that George was more liberal minded; quite simply, she was the apple of his eye and could twist him round her little finger. The proof of this pudding lay in the way that he immediately let her into the bedroom; now in a bit of a state. Debbie gawped in astonishment at laboratory paraphernalia that littered the floor. Test-tubes, bunsen burners, pipettes, burettes, retorts, crucibles plus jars full of different coloured crystals and dark grey powder. George refused to explain why he had opened his son's Megaton Chemistry Set.

"I thought that was for Anthony on Christmas day."

Her father didn't seem to care. Totally distracted, eyes bulging like a mad scientist, all he wanted was two pounds of sugar, electric wiring and a can of weed-killer from the garage. Debbie didn't understand the purpose of his bizarre request but agreed to anything when he promised not to object in any way, shape or form to her latest boyfriend. He nodded but she didn't know if he was really listening. George picked up a hammer and a cylindrical object made of lead with wires oddly sticking out.

"What are you making?" she asked tentatively.

"Nothing."

"Well, what's it for?"

"Revenge," mumbled her father.

He moaned about how badly they treated him at the Head Office of Midshires Building Society and how much he hated his Boss, Investment Department Manager, Mr William H. Brown. It was all unspoken but he knew they thought he was an old fashioned bore with his double chin, podgy face and green cardigan with knobbly buttons. He had recently been passed over for promotion in favour of much younger colleagues with far less experience. A sneaky midget called Martin Marriott, a goggle-eyed freak called Steve Powell and a pompous idiot called Geoff Richardson who were considered by aforementioned Manager to be trendy, dynamic, financial whiz-kids in sleek Armani suits. George finished his tirade by muttering one name to himself over and over again: "Bill Brown, Bill Brown, Bill Brown, Bill Brown, Bill Brown…" Debbie left the bedroom during this perverse mantra shaking her head in despair. Christmas Day at 42 Eastfield Street was going to be like any other day. Dead miserable.

There was little sense of excitement in the living room. Arthur had dropped off to sleep and Sheila was diligently wiping saliva off his chin. She was very annoyed… It wasn't her responsibility to look after Arthur. That was his wife's job but Enid just sat in the armchair making sarcastic remarks.

"What are we having for Christmas dinner, boil in the bag chicken curry?

Sheila managed to control herself; yes, so easy to blow her top but that would be playing into Enid's hands. The woman in black twisted the knife in further.

"Look at that pattern on the wallpaper. It looks like you've squashed dead spiders on the wall."

She guffawed at her own joke then belched. Sheila smiled through gritted teeth, stood up and walked stiffly out of the room.

Sheila was dimly aware of a faint tap, tap, tapping noise originating from upstairs. However, she placed it on the back burner because the nigh impossibility of inserting a large, awkwardly shaped turkey into the oven was simmering on the front. She took the plunge; approached the oven holding the 27lb beast then attempted to squeeze it in. Whilst engaged in this pressing activity her seventeen years old son, Anthony, lurched through the back door, bounced off a cupboard, fell to his knees and retched into the pedal bin...

Out of her mind with worry Sheila dropped the turkey and cradled her poor, sick child in her arms. Seconds later she reeled from alcoholic fumes emanating from every pore in his body and gave him the mother of all mouthfuls. The accused immediately pleaded guilty. Anthony admitted he was drunk for the first time in his life and burst into tears. Sheila abandoned any remaining maternal instincts and began to throttle him. To escape from her clutches he flapped, twisted and rolled away... Anthony staggered to his feet incoherently slurring it wasn't his fault, then, slightly more compos mentis, feebly explained that he'd been duped by older and wiser mates. Well, he thought they were wiser until they lured him into a series of unfortunate accidents... In spite of his mother's incredulity Anthony continued with the likely story of how they'd ended up at 'The Flying Pig's Karaoke Evening' where, while he was warbling 'Are you lonesome, tonight?' his twenty three stone mate, Dennis, wept like a baby then picked him up and twirled him round over the top of his head. The combination of drink and helicopter spinning motion made Anthony vomit over the gold embossed, leather bound request book with each laminated page protected by a plastic jacket. Mr David Davenport, of 'Dave's Karaoke' renown, was a trifle upset and thumped him in the face. Sheila's inspection of the lovely black eye which marred her son's boyish good looks was interrupted by, well, at first she thought she was seeing things....

The apparition in the kitchen was a young man, unsteady on high heels, wearing dark blue eye shadow, coral lipstick and an elegant, full length turquoise gown. Moreover, he sported spiky blonde hair and on his face, chest and arms tattooed designs which would have fooled the untrained eye into believing were esoteric, Masonic or even cabbalistic signs. Sheila was repulsed and fascinated at the same time.

"Oh, yeah. This is my mate, Sam," said Anthony.

"What?"

Sheila could hardly hear him with the relentless bang, bang, banging din from upstairs. After Anthony shouted his name she stared with a strange, vacuous smile on her face. Not for the first time this evening Sheila was speechless. Whatever it was had a sensible suggestion for the relief of Anthony's throbbing face.

"Why don't you put a steak on his eye?"

She didn't have a steak but Sam thought a turkey would do just as well.

"Oh, why bother?" replied Sheila. "We'll be late with tomorrow's dinner, anyway. We'll have to eat after the Queen's speech instead of before."

She tossed the turkey to her son. Anthony held it to his face while his mother complained about his father's inconsiderate, anti-social behaviour. When he realised that Sam had disappeared he began to panic and Sheila stopped in full flow.

"What's the matter?"

"I have to watch Sam every second when he's pissed. He's liable to seduce everything in sight."

Anthony ran out of the kitchen leaving his baffled mother talking to thin air.

"But all that revolting make-up and he's wearing a dress!"

The hammering ceased and a scream of pain, like a water buffalo being castrated, rang through the house. Sheila entered the living room and witnessed a scene from a pornographic horror movie; Sam astride Enid voraciously sucking and slobbering on her blotchy, triple-chinned face. Obviously, from a generation unfamiliar with dangereuse lesbian liaisons Enid went bright red in outrage which knew no bounds. A girl in a dress was kissing her and that was that! She summoned up considerable strength and rose from the armchair like a kraken from the deep. Poor Sam, taken by surprise, was thrown across the room and the back of his head crashed against the wall. He just lay there in a drunken daze, wasted eyes rolling... Any attempt at a rational explanation would have been pointless. Enid failed to comprehend anything; simply couldn't believe that Anthony, her little nephew, had been allowed to fraternize with a deeply disturbed pervert. Sheila, sick to death of her undermining jibes, took umbrage and told Enid to mind her own business in no uncertain terms. A ding-dong argument ensued until Anthony stamped his feet and shouted incomprehensibly in a voice oscillating between bass, tenor and falsetto. Enid did a double take at the sight of her precious, little nephew, who had mutated into a turkey-headed blasphemy, before resorting to the easier target of her husband's abject failure to defend her honour.

"That's typical, Arthur. Absolutely typical! Yes, you just sat there like a zombie staring at the ceiling. I should have expected it. A pathetic, drooling, idiot, stupid zombie!" She burst into tears. "And you were no help, either!"

Enid jabbed a stumpy finger at her niece who had turned as white as a sheet. Sheila kneeled on the shag-pile carpet, wrung her hands and stared at her daughter. She was most concerned; Debbie's trembling body and ghost-like face indicated that something was drastically wrong.

"What's the matter, babe? Are you feeling poorly?"

"No."

"Well, you don't look very well. Are you sure you're alright?"

"Yes."

"Not sickening for anything?"

"No."

"Is it your father? Has your father upset you?" "No."

"You've not been drinking, have you? Oh, God! Not you as well."

"No!"

"Are you sure?"

"Yes."

Sheila sucked her giblet flavoured fingernail.

"Well, if you're not poorly and it's not your father and it's not the drink. What on earth is it?"

"Nothing."

Debbie put her head in her hands and wept. Her mother's endless, rapid-fire questions had inevitably worn her down.

"Are you in some kind of trouble?"

"Yes. I'm pregnant!"

Debbie just blurted it out then helpfully added a vital piece of information; the father was in this very room. Sheila's jaw dropped open in whodunit astonishment as her eyes probed the prime suspects. The first recovering his dignity in a rather fetching turquoise number, second an anorak cousin glued to the telly, third a slobbering, speechless Uncle and the fourth was a gawky younger brother and they weren't living in Norfolk. She shook her head in despair; it dawned upon her that she wasn't Miss Marple or Hercule Poirot in the library. Absolutely clueless, Sheila resorted to firing another series of questions at her tearful, distraught daughter. Her volume gradually increased until Wayne crawled across the shag-pile, cocked his ear to the telly and nerdily protested that he couldn't hear the Cybermen hissing insidious threats to Rose, Doctor Who's beautiful, blonde assistant. Anthony, unable to get a word in edgeways, thumped the frozen turkey in sheer frustration while pacing up and down in an agitated state.

"You're my best friend… Yes, and you went…" were the inconsequential words he eventually squealed. He leapt in front of Sam. "Oh, Christ! Not with… No! Don't tell me you had the bloody nerve…"

Never before had Sam faced the dire consequences of his promiscuous behaviour. It was a bit of a blow; he was unnerved when these murky revelations bubbled to the surface and squirmed with embarrassment when Debbie threw her milky white arms around him.

"Yes, it's true. I'm having Sam's baby."

Enid laughed like a drain. "Don't be silly, Debbie. You can't get pregnant by another girl."

Sheila had one of her panic attacks. She breathed quickly with limbs jerking spasmodically in adult parody of funky, robotic dance moves. Outside, on the pavement, a Salvation Army band played the opening bars of 'Silent Night.' Sheila thrust open the window and shouted, "For God's sake, shut up!" Unfortunately, the brass band had formed a circle and could neither see nor hear her so, infuriated at being ignored, she slammed the window shut. Meanwhile, Anthony was trying to ascertain the true gender, sexual inclination of his erstwhile friend.

"Transvestite, transsexual, bisexual, heterosexual or homosexual?"

Sam shrugged. "I just like wearing women's clothes."

"Do you know Big John Cassidy?"

"Who?"

"The guy with the orange and yellow mohican who's covered in satanic tattoos?"

"Erm… Yes."

"Why were you kissing him in 'The Flying Pig,' tonight?"

The proverbial stuff hit the fan. Debbie slapped Sam's face and, near hysterical, screamed that the wedding was off! That it had been on was a surprise to everyone apart from cousin Wayne who was more interested in the galactic fate of Doctor Who's beautiful, blonde assistant. Debbie sobbed into her sopping handkerchief twittering she wished she'd never clapped eyes on Sam because he was a complete bastard who had ruined her life. Enid placed a thick, protective arm around her waist and, as if addressing a backward five year old, instructed her on the rudiments of one girl not being allowed to marry another girl. Anthony plucked up the courage to inform his formidable Aunt that nowadays she couldn't in Church but could in a Registry Office. Enid fixed him with a black, menacing stare. His attempt to summarize New Labour's change in the law ended in tongue-tied confusion. She continued staring… Sheila, whose blood curdled at the prospect of such a hellish marriage, ran to the door and yelled for George to come down. It was all too much for Debbie. She threatened to kill herself by sticking her head in the oven but her mother forbad it.

"There's no room for your head. I've got to put the turkey in there."

Debbie was furious at having to postpone her suicide attempt. Well out of control, she wrestled the turkey from Anthony's clutches and hurled it through the front window. Before anybody could react a deafening explosion shook the house to its foundations. Half of the ceiling collapsed and George dropped through the gaping hole and landed on the carpet. He was covered in bricks, dust and plaster and incessantly moaning, "Bill Brown, Bill Brown, Bill Brown, Bill Brown…" Everyone was suffering from shock except Wayne who asked, "What's happened to the picture?" Men in distinctive blue and red uniforms were clambering through the smashed window. Under the mistaken impression that the Third World War had started Enid wondered if they were from Civil Defence.

"No, love. We're the Salvation Army."

The pandemonium subsided. George appeared to be the only serious casualty and three Christian soldiers transformed into angelic nurses cradling his head, checking for broken bones and holding his hand. Another one dialled nine-nine-nine and in a clear, lucid style reported a major incident at 42 Eastfield street. For several minutes nobody spoke. It was an utterly strange atmosphere. A stillness after the storm permeated the living room while they recovered what was left of their wits until a squeaky voice piped up:

"If everyone loved each other there would be peace and hope in the world."

Arthur had spoken. He looked around with a silly, fatuous grin on his face. The whole family were astonished. Anthony, who'd studied

GCSE psychology, thought the explosion must have shocked Arthur out of his trauma. The Salvation Army were on their knees praying; convinced they had witnessed another miracle. Outside, an ambulance siren wailed…

A FEW PEARS TOO MANY

Rose Aitken

"We don't need a house this big." I told Sandra on the day we went to look at the place. I mean, this place made big look inadequate as a term. Talk about rambling. I tell you, if this house had legs it would ramble for miles and not even stop for a drink of water at a crystal stream. It had a fine old orchard at the back which sprawled rather in the manner of a beer drinking, pipe smoking bachelor after a fine lunch. There were trees everywhere. Plum, apple, peach and even pear. There were fruit bushes too. Loads of them. My fingers quaked at the mere thought of pruning that lot. Thank god Sandra would have to do it. There were gooseberries and black currants all over the place. There were more raspberry canes than I could count.

"Well I think it's nice. We can really live here."

"Get lost you mean. It'll be like a route march just getting from one bedroom to another. As for the garden. Well, I hear the marines are looking for a place to perform military manoeuvres in. We could hire this garden out."

"Don't be ridiculous." My dear lady wife stood on the sunny porch step, hands on hips and ruling over all she surveyed even though we hadn't signed any paperwork yet. I could see her now. Garden shears in hand, bending the will of every plant and thing that moved to her desire. It almost looked to me standing there that the very black currant bushes visibly quaked at the prospect of those garden shears. I knew how they felt. I'd done my share of quaking in my time with my dear lady wife as well. Now though I just nodded and said yes dear a few times and hoped for the best.

"Are you sure you can manage all this acreage?" I had to try one last time to dissuade her from embarking on this ludicrous project. "I mean, you could fit Windsor Castle and Clarence House in one corner of this place."

Sandra gave me that look which sent me scuttling out of reach. "It's my money that's paying for this and yes I am sure. I'll cope and if I can't I'll hire some of the locals to help with the more arduous tasks."

"There is a local man who does the trees," the dithery little clerk from the estate agent told her with a sickly smile at me.

I wanted to knock his head off his shoulders for that but I didn't dare. Not with Sandra standing closer than me. Don't misunderstand me. My dear lady wife isn't really a dragon. She drove all the dragons away years ago. They got scared of her. Her fire breathing exploits put them all to shame so they left town in disgrace and were never seen again. Well, who could blame them for steering clear of my dear lady wife? You see my dear wife had flame red hair and green eyes rather than green fingers, though she has those as well after a day among the plants which is a lethal combination in any case. I think I must have had one or two whiskies too many on the night I proposed to her, though why Sandra accepted I do not know unless it might have been because she knew how miserable I'd be afterwards. Well serves me right.

Sandra had inherited a small fortune from some uncle who I'd never met and now this dear woman who breathed fire everywhere intended to spend it on the home of her dreams. The mere fact that this ideal home happened to be a mansion, castle and manor house all rolled together and added to a bit had nothing to do with it. You could really get lost in this place. Unless that happened to be her intention. Mind you, there might be advantages to a place this big. I could get right out of her way. Suddenly the idea didn't seem so bad after all.

"All right dear," I agreed. "If you really want it I'll go along with you."

Sandra gave me another paint blistering look. "Of course you will. You'll do as you're told. In any case I don't recall asking your opinion." She turned to the clerk. "We'll take it. Where's the contract?"

The bloody oaf produced it! Right there on the porch step of our new colossus. Sandra speed read the details and signed. "You'll have the cheque by Monday. Is that all right?" Sandra gave him a velvet smile which had steel underneath.

"Oh that'll be fine madam. I'll tell Mr. Smythe."

So the house became ours. We moved during the summer. One single van. Our poor furniture would be helplessly lost in such a place. I assumed we'd shut some of it up but I didn't reckon on my dear wife. She had other plans for our new palace.

"I want all the rooms decorated in different styles. I want a morning room and a reception room. I also want guest rooms fully equipped."

"But we don't get that many visitors," I protested. I just about refrained from asking if she wanted an afternoon and evening room as well. My life wouldn't have been worth living if I'd given in to temptation so I didn't.

"We will. I've got plans for our new home."

"What're you gonna do? Turn it in to a hotel or something?"

"Don't be so vulgar Peter. This is our home. I don't want guests cluttering up the place unless I know them. Anyway there's too much stealing goes on in hotels. I don't want light fingered thieves running all over the place."

"Thank heavens for that," I muttered. I knew who'd be chief cook and bottle washer if my dear lady wife wanted to fill the house with guests. I'd end up being the bloody chamber maid as well, my gender notwithstanding.

At last we got settled. The decorators were there all through that summer and well in to the autumn. Sandra spent all her energy and time in the garden planting and weeding. We did get in some local help. An old guy called Reg attended to the trees.

"They'll do well this year," the guy once informed me in a broad Devon accent. "Plenty of fruit. You'll get some good cider outa them apples."

"Cider?" I queried.

"There be a cider press down in the cellar. Haven't you bin down there yet?"

The guy had to be joking. As if this place didn't have enough rooms in it already now he goes and tells me there's a cellar with a cider press of all things.

I told Sandra this later that day as we sat eating buttered scones, made by Doris our new cook, in our echoing dining room. To my utter surprise Sandra seemed to take to the idea of making cider at once. I still don't know what made me tell her about it.

"Won't that be fun? No more vat on drink. We can make our own!"

"Aren't there laws about such things?"

Sandra snorted which I knew spelled trouble. "Only if you get caught doing it. How many government officials have you seen around here lately?"

"Well you've never done this sort of thing before." I don't know why I bother to try to discourage her but I do. Masochism I suppose. Oh well.

Sandra agreed to that. "But there's always a first time. How hard can it be?"

I didn't know. "I just hope the whole place doesn't explode while you learn."

"The trouble with you Peter is that you are altogether too melodramatic. Of course the place won't explode. Have I ever set fire to anything yet?"

I almost said yes. The kitchen when she'd gone out to pay the milkman, got chatting about cows, and almost let the chip pan catch fire. However I held my peace. If I hadn't you wouldn't be reading this now. I have learned over the years when to hold my tongue and that is most of the time.

Well the fruit started rolling in later that September. There were plums galore. There were sack loads of apples. Doris started bringing in all the bottles she could find. The whole kitchen stank of fruit. Jars and jars of apple and plum jam stood on shelves in the pantry. I didn't see my dear lady wife for days. Apparently her enquiries had elicited Reg's help again in the matter of cider. Well, the old boy could stay with her as long as there were hours in a day if he could handle her. As it happened the old boy could. They got along so well I started to feel left out.

Then came the pears. Bucket loads of them and that didn't count the windfalls which we gave to the kids who passed on their way up to the moors or to school.

We ate pears for lunch, pears for dinner and even pears for breakfast. We had pear pie, pear crumble, pears with sauce and even just on their own.

"We'll 'ave to do somethin' with this lot before they go bad," Reg told us as he lugged yet another basket of the damn things in to our overflowing kitchen. Even the dining room didn't echo so much now.

The damn place positively burst with bloody boxes of fruit. I kept falling over the stuff.

"There's enough to feed an army here," I complained.

"What can we do with it all?" Even Sandra had reached her wits' end by now.

"We could try making cider with them. They might do well at that."

"Can you make pear cider?"

"Who'll drink it all?" I added.

"You could sell it to the locals. That's what the old squire used to do." Reg's eyes lit up with the memory. "They won't tell. They likes their cider if it's made right."

"And you know how?" I queried.

"I makes the best cider in the district if not in the land. Just leave it to old Reg."

So we did. The old boy spent every day down in the cellar. I helped him carry the fruit down there and he did the rest.

"Of course," the old boy told us one day while we were having breakfast – Reg often joined us now since he started work so early in the morning, "there's the honey too. There's two dozen hives down at the bottom of the garden. You'll 'ave plenty for the winter. It's good honey too. I knows the bee keeper."

We groaned simultaneously. "We've seen no bee keeper," we said in unison. Actually I'd seen some guy dressed in a white suit but I'd put it down to some local yokel in eccentric mood and so for once hadn't told Sandra.

"That's coz 'e keeps 'imself to 'imself. 'E's a nice old chap. A bit dozy but that's nothin' wrong wi' that. Then there's all the soft fruit.

You know the blackberries and black currants and so forth. What'll you do with them?"

"How the hell should I know?" Sandra exploded. "What do you suggest?"

"They makes good wine and the gooseberries go down well with the kids. They loves their gooseberries." It amazed me that old Reg could not only sit there facing my dear lady wife but he even answered her totally unperturbed by her loss of temper. I didn't know whether to envy him or hate him.

"Well all right. If you say so."

Later that day Sandra cornered me in what she now referred to as the library though for what possible reason I do not know. It didn't contain books.

"Do you remember that suggestion of yours to open this place and turn it in to a hotel?" She gave me a smile which made me wary.

I forbore to mention that I hadn't suggested it at all. I'd merely asked what her intentions were. I nodded. "What about it?"

"Well, if we do up the front parlour we could open it up as a pub couldn't we? That way we could sell our cider legitimately and get rid of some of it."

"What about the law? We'd have to charge vat."

"No we wouldn't. I've had a word with Reg and he says we could move all the bottles out once the cider's ready and show the officials who grant the licences an empty room. Then they'll never know that we do a sideline in cider. We could sell the beer and so on legitimately and do the cider as an added extra to preferred customers. That way that pesky government of ours won't get all the tax."

I thought it a bit risky myself especially as I had something to tell her. However, because I value my skin I let it pass.

So the idea took shape as autumn became winter and winter became spring. Then came the news which I had, over the weeks, come to dread. Our application for a licence had been approved. The inspectors had come and given the place the once over and all had gone well. Now all we needed were a name for the place and some customers. Still, I couldn't feel happy.

Naturally Sandra noticed my lack of enthusiasm. She quizzed me about it one day while we were doing our morning military exercises from the bedroom down to the dining room. At least five miles as the crow flies.

"What's up with you then?"

"Oh nothing. It's just that I've got a new job within the civil service department. We might have to move or stop this venture of yours."

She turned to me her eyes blazing mad. "Why should we do that?"

"Because we might have to."

"What is this new job of yours then? What is it you do that means you can no longer commute to work as you've been doing?"

"I'm a tax inspector. I'd have to report you for tax evasion."

"Not bloody likely. I'll start divorce procedures if you so much as dare."

A rock and a hard place. Isn't that what they call it? The devil and the deep blue sea. I didn't mind the prospect of cheap booze and I wouldn't mind the escape from Sandra that my new job offered. Still I didn't think so badly of her to report her for tax evasion. What to do? I had no idea. In the end I merely turned a blind eye. With the money we were soon making it wouldn't matter if I lost my job or not. It failed to dawn on me at the time that we wouldn't be making so much if Sandra lost her licence as well. However, to date that hasn't happened. Now we have more honey then we can eat and the pear trees continue to do well. We are coining it in since most of the locals drink cider anyway and Sandra is kept too busy to annoy me so I'm thoroughly drunk and thoroughly happy. What utter bliss.

MADEIRA

Wendy Edmond

Cinnamon and Oak
shade the old Quinta among
rich orchards and vines.

Across lawns and through
an aisle of columnar pines
to Columbo's den.

The giant tortoise
likes mango, pineapple, grapes,
juice drips from his chin.

A fountain splashes
where the pied doves stoop to drink
in dappled sunlight.

Amber, black-latticed
monarch butterflies dancing
in the shade at noon.

Where lovers murmur
in the scented lemon grove,
the garden listens.

A patch of earth shifts,
a hundred basking geckos
break for cover.

Swans gliding over
dark water, strewn with lilies,
above darting koi.

Dinner by moonlight,
a canopy of jasmine
on the verandah.

Rain, at dead of night,
rushing past the balcony
as a waterfall.

DIALOGUE...

Eva Ziebicki

'Is anyone at home?' bellowed a man's voice 'Let me see you if you're half decent.'

'Wait a minute, I'm coming right now.' I felt excited. 'Is that you, Bill?... You rang the way you used to sometimes.'

'I rang three times. One long, two short.'

'So you're back then.'

'The great wanderer returns.'

'Why are you here?'

'I wanted to see how you were, how much you'd grown.'

'Very funny!'

Bill's eyes lit up. 'You're beautiful.'

I felt embarrassed.

'You might as well come in but you can't stay for long... I'm off out soon.'

'I'm elated, just seeing you... Never thought you'd invite me into your house.'

'I'm not sure I'm going to...'

'Marjorie...'

'Oh, Come on then. We can't just stand here looking like sheep. Mind the step... I've decorated, with Magnolia throughout and dusty pink in the lounge. It's fresh.'

...You could breathe in the freshness.

'I'll make a pot of tea', I said.

'I'd like that.'He hesitated. Look love…'

'You don't have to say anything at all…'

'I do, Marjorie, I do.'

'I don't want an argument, Bill.'

'And neither do I.'

'Canada must be lovely', I said.

'Toronto's great. Wide, open spaces, clubs…'

I poured the tea.

'We had a summer house on the lake. There were wild animals, skunks and grizzly bears. You could go fishing. We ate fresh produce regularly. It's a clean life.'

'Are you still with Tracy?'

Both of us sat quiet for a while.

'How's the country dancing?' Bill replied coolly.

'Ballroom dancing still gives me a buzz. Brings up the goose pimples before competitions.'

'So, you're still doing those, then?'

'Yes', I said.'Like the good old days.'

'Good for you!'

Silence.

'How's Jennifer?'

'Fine. There's so much catching up for you to do if you're interested...she's moved on, grown- up now.'

I said, 'She's moved out, got her own flat and a young man. Good sort. Biscuit? Your favourite.'

Bill declined.

Silence.

'We've been through hell.'

'I know...'

'Bill if only you knew and quite frankly, here you come, swanning into my house, naturally with my permission, which I've had to struggle to keep together with Jennifer's help. Here you are, a great-bronzed Spanish looking bloke with your shirt wide-open and wearing your prize winning medallion, appearing as if you've just been on your holiday. I've heard you're rolling in it. Sorry, Bill but I've got to say how I feel. I never did, but after all these years.'

'It's all right love.'

'What! Why aren't you in flipping Canada where you should be? I heard you've got a yacht and all that.'

'I've got two; we had two. One of them is on the market. I'm selling up. I've come home. I'm here now. Have you had the chance to see my dog?'

'Dog! You've got a dog!'

'Yep, a king-sized poodle.' Bill grinned widely like I'd never seen before.

'I can't keep up with you, honest. What about Canada! I realise how little I know about anywhere.'

'I want to give you some money', Bill said.

'What!'

'Let me speak, Marjorie. I've been foolish and you've been through a lot both of you, you and Jen; more than most. Don't think I've not realised all that, I have. Everything happened all at once, the money, the move. Yep, I won some cash and yes I moved away. I had a contract out in Toronto. The date was set and Tracy booked the flight, as my secretary. She had experience as a typist and all that. We row a lot, Marjorie.'

And then Bill took out a chequebook and scribbled.

Thursday must have been my lucky day.

'You may not accept this, but…'

'I accept your money. I accept whatever you want to give me. Thank you', I said.

THE WARDROBE

Muir Sperrings

Scrolled handles on creamy veneer
with dark swirling orbs that stare
round edged proportions tall and grand
overflow with an awkward air

The eyes are all seeing - come closer
as red chiffon cuffs on a blouse
beckon through the half open door
to anyone daring to browse

One step in; and the curious
laden hangers crowd around
pushing and shoving as they do
just to annoy and to confound

A trace of lavender seeps through
when linen folds embrace and
silk brushes cheek at the parting
in the rain on the lonely moorland

In the darkness of the corner
a delightful shiver occurs
of touch upon green velvet
as a past memory lingers

Fingers caress black horsehair plaits
their spiral forms lovingly wrought
she had lived on clover pastures
and died with a kiss - one shot

Shelved just above the heaving throng
the neatly folded garments, moan
as one by one they are pulled aside
or impatiently thrown out, alone

Underneath lie an assortment
of boxes plain and satin lined
in one, two broken silver pens
and others, jewels that a throat entwined

Close by, leaning against the back
is a smoothly dark fur neckpiece
with a clasp that holds it all in place
a favourite, a genuine timepiece

The intrusion has worked a treat
everything is back as before
a feeling of satisfaction
on both sides of the still open door

GOING HOME

Jenny Evans

I left the main road behind me and walked into the dimly lit side street, just as I did every day after work. The difference between the two areas never failed to surprise me. If it hadn't been for the row of cars parked along the side of the cobbled road, I could have stepped back in time, just by turning the corner.

The street was a dead end and lined with mature trees which were just starting to lose their leaves. On one side was a row of Victorian terraced houses that had seen better days, which were mostly used as office space now. On the other side was a cemetery wall, its blank canvas still untouched by the graffiti artists. Maybe this road was just a little too far off the beaten track for them. It was the sort of area where you half expected to see horse-drawn carriages, and maybe a lamplighter making his way along.

I pulled my coat up closer round my neck as the autumnal air started to worm its way under the fabric, and headed towards my car which was parked at the end of the cul-de-sac. I could still make out the far off traffic noise, but it seemed to hang in the stillness, as if wrapped in cotton wool. The evening had a strange, surreal feel to it, a bit like an old familiar dream. Not threatening or unfriendly, but actually quite welcoming.

As I walked along the damp pavement the dim street lights became further and further apart. Maybe it was my imagination but the noise of my boots seemed to become louder as the night became darker. They also seemed to be creating an echo. Click-click, click-click, they went. I took to walking very slowly and deliberately, trying not to make any noise at all, but the extra click was always there. I even tried walking on tip-toe but that didn't seem to make any difference either. Eventually I stopped moving completely and waited. 'Click' I heard behind me.

I spun round expecting to see someone following me, but the noise stopped and there was no-one there. Giving myself a mental kick up the backside for having an over-fertile imagination, I turned back and carried on walking.

Immediately the click-clicking started again. I stopped and swung round. Squinting into the darkness I searched about for someone, but there was nothing to be seen.

"Hello," I said, and then louder, "who's there?" No response came from the cotton wool silence. "I know someone's there, what's the problem?" Still nothing. "Fine, please yourself," and off I set again.

I was moving faster now, but the footsteps behind me were still there and seemed to be getting louder. I kept checking over my shoulder but there was no-one to be seen, and by this time I was starting to feel anxious and more than a little scared.

Almost running the last few yards to my car, I began scrabbling around in my handbag, cursing the lack of pockets in it. The clicking was getting nearer now, and I just didn't have the nerve to turn and confront whoever was behind me. All I wanted to do was get into the safety of my car and shut out this unseen presence.

Finding the bunch of keys buried at the bottom of my bag, I fumbled with immobile fingers, trying to get the right one into the lock.

“Come on,” I muttered under my breath.

Suddenly the key slid in. I turned it and the car was at last undone, but as I went to open the door the keys slipped from my hand and dropped out of sight.

Swearing to myself, I crouched down and frantically started groping about on the wet ground under the car. Eventually my fingertips touched the key fob, but it was just out of reach so I knelt down on the gritty pavement and grabbed it. Edging back, I was about to get up when a small movement caught my eye.

Bending down further and looking under the car I could see someone standing there. It was obviously a man, and he was wearing a pair of heavy, old-fashioned black boots.

Cowering by the side of the car, clutching my handbag and keys, I felt the weakness of fear and panic take hold of me. I had absolutely no idea what to do and my body seemed incapable of movement. My heart was thumping so hard it literally felt as if it might explode out of my chest. Taking deep breaths to try and calm myself, I looked again under the car. The feet were still there, they didn’t seem to have moved at all.

Half crawling, I inched my way round to the front of the vehicle, then alongside the bonnet. My breath was pumping as fast as my heart and I was sure that my assailant – if that’s what he was – must be able to hear it. I paused and listened for any sound of movement, but there was none, so steeling myself I very carefully peered round the side of the car.

Nothing. There was nothing there. There was no-one there. Where had he gone? He was there, and then he wasn’t there. I couldn’t have imagined it. Could I?

I stood slowly and leaning against the car I scanned around, but all I could see were all the things I would have expected to see. Just other cars and buildings and the dim street lights. Certainly no bogey men lurking in the shadows. My breathing began to subside and the weakness in my legs slowly disappeared.

"Okay, its fine," I said out loud, breaking the claustrophobic silence, "nothing there. It's fine, all fine. Imagination, that's all."

Anxious to be safely inside the car, I picked up my handbag that had somehow dropped to the floor and opened the driver's door. Suddenly there was an ear-piercing screech and something brushed past my legs, knocking me off balance. I spun round, just in time to see a black and white cat disappearing over the wall into the graveyard. Bubbles of laughter rose in my throat, ready to pop out at any moment.

"This must be what hysteria feels like," I thought. Then out loud, "Get a grip girl."

Sliding my body into the driver's seat, I pulled the door shut with a comforting thud, locked the doors, and sat for a few moments trying to calm down. Putting the key in the ignition, I started the engine and turned the radio on. A man's voice cut into the silence,

"Come on Tony my friend," he was saying, "tell us all about it then. What happened when you came out of the shower and found all your clothes were missing?"

One of the late night DJs was having a jokey conversation with an unsuspecting punter, who was about to be made the butt of some inane joke. This was the sort of mindless programme that I usually hated, but was actually just what I needed at that moment.

Before putting the car into gear I reached behind me for my seat belt, and then checked my mirror before indicating to pull away. I always do that, even when I know there can't be anything coming. Old habits die hard. Mirror, signal, manoeuvre.

But this time I didn't indicate, and I didn't pull away. There in my mirror was the reflection of a man's face. Timeless somehow, with piercing blue eyes and heavy brows, he was staring back at me from the rear seat. Cold panic rushed up through my body, and I could feel my throat starting to close up.

The doors were locked; I knew I'd locked them, so how could this be? I let go of my unfastened seat belt and stared back at him, as if mesmerised. His unblinking eyes seemed to cut right through me.

A voice I barely recognised as my own said quietly, "Who are you? What do you want?"

Without taking his eyes away from mine, the man replied, "You, Rebecca Ann Daws. I want you."

Filled with horror, I whispered, "But you don't know me."

"Oh I know you very well," he said quietly, "you are mine."

Looking down, I stared at my white knuckles still gripping the steering wheel. My hands dropped onto my lap, and I registered that some of my nails were broken and the varnish chipped. The DJ started talking again and this seemed to jolt me out of my inertia, and filled me with an enormous fury.

"No," I shouted, finding my voice again, "I am not yours." Then remembering something Simon once told me about defending myself, I yanked the key out of the ignition, jumped out of the car, and pulled open the back door. Prepared to attack.

No-one was there. The seat was cold and empty, and there was no evidence that anyone had been sitting there only moments earlier. A loud buzzing sound started in my head and my legs almost gave way under me. Slamming the rear door shut, I fell back into my seat and pushed the key back into the ignition, before blackness swallowed me up.

I've no idea how long I passed out for, but I was brought back to consciousness by the sound of the radio. For a few moments I was totally disorientated and couldn't remember what had happened, and why I was sitting in my car. Then the panic came flooding back. Starting the engine, and jamming the car into gear, I screeched off up the road, up towards the safety of other traffic and people.

I knew I was driving much too fast, but all I could think was that I had to get home. Every red light that stopped me was cause for alarm. I was scared to look in my rear view mirror, afraid of what I might see.

I tried to get my mobile out of my bag, but my fingers wouldn't work properly. The idea was to ring Simon and tell him what had happened, but how could I explain it. Would I say that there had been a man in my car, but then he wasn't there? It sounded so stupid. I decided to just concentrate on getting home safely and tell him all about it then. He'd give me a big hug and explain it all away, and I'd feel safe. That was all I wanted, to feel safe.

The DJ on the radio was now chatting away to another unfortunate soul about a swimming trunk malfunction, and I was starting to feel a bit calmer. My heart was not beating so fast, and the buzzing in my head seemed to be subsiding. At some point I even sang along to Gloria Gaynor's 'I Will Survive," which made me laugh out loud.

Nearing home, I realised that I was hungry and that I'd had nothing to eat since a cheese and pickle sandwich at lunchtime. Pulling into the parking bay outside the fish and chip shop, I nipped inside and got two cod and chips. Even if Simon had already eaten he could always find room for a bit extra, as proven by his slightly expanding waistband.

As I set off I suddenly realised that I'd looked in my rear view mirror when I'd pulled away from the parking spot, and more importantly – there was no-one there. Relief flooded through me, and my mood lifted dramatically. By the time I pulled into our driveway I was feeling much more like my normal self, and when the DJ started winding up his next victim I turned off the ignition in disgust.

The smell of the fish was permeating the car, and I needed to get the meal into the oven to keep warm. But first I knew I had to look once again in the mirror, just to be sure.

Forcing myself, I raised my eyes to look into the darkness behind me, and again there was nothing there. I was home, and I was safe. Whatever terrors I had imagined were gone, left behind, never to be repeated.

I got out of the car and locked it. Balancing the paper parcel of food and my handbag on one arm, I managed to open our front door. Apart from the small light in the hallway, the house was in darkness.

"Simon, I'm back," I shouted, "sorry I'm a bit late." But there was no reply. Walking into the kitchen, I switched on the oven and popped the food in to keep warm. "Strange," I thought. Then I spotted the note leaning on the kettle.

Hi Beccs. Got called into work, some emergency. Hopefully won't be too long, but will ring if I'm going to be late. Don't worry about food for me.

S xx

"Looks like the dog next door is going to get a treat," I thought to myself, envisaging the mountain of chips currently residing in the oven.

I dumped my coat and bag on the kitchen table and made my way round the house closing curtains and turning on a few lights. Switching on the television I noticed that there had been a crowd of youngsters running riot in the town centre earlier. Shop windows had been broken and extra police had been drafted in. "That explains the missing husband," I thought. "Oh well, meal for one in front of the box it will have to be."

Back in the kitchen I got my tray set up, and was just about to get the food out of the oven when the phone started to ring. "That'll be him," I thought. Picking it up, I said, "Hello. Oh hi. Yes I just saw it on the news. What's going on?" As Simon was telling about what was happening, I reached up to close the roller blind at the kitchen window.

My body went cold and the hairs on the back of my neck stood on end. There behind me, reflected in the glass, was a man with heavy brows and piercing blue eyes. As the blackness once again overtook me, the last sound I heard was Tony saying "Beccs, are you ok?" before the phone smashed as it hit the kitchen floor.

VAUGHAN WRITERS

MUSIC MAN

Eva Ziebicki

Her eyes sparkled as he turned
to look at her.

He shook his head, and looked towards the ground
"I really can't explain," he said

If all he wanted to do was talk about his piano recital
...then we could have briefly met for a coffee and left,

Because that's how I feel

"I know this isn't making a lot of sense," she said

So he sang her a love song,

And she excused herself, reached out for her purse bag

And made for the door….

RISING TO THE CHALLENGE

Sheila Lockett

I thought I ought to try a gym
lose weight, get fit and slim.
I joined a ladies only one
and hoped I'd soon be thin.
Think positive.

The members were all ages
wore joggers and tee shirts
no skinny birds in leotards
who only like to flirt.
Thank goodness.

First they weighed and measured me
then handed me a chart
so I could record my scores,
then it was time to start.
Here goes.

There were a lot of toning chairs
designed to keep you trim.
You push your legs, pull your arms
and hold your stomach in.
Such a strain.

Next ten minutes on the bike,
the treadmill and the rower,
then the dreaded cross trainer
I'm starting to get slower.
It's exhausting.

Time once again for measuring
It's ten weeks since I started,
no inches lost and two lbs on
I'm feeling so downhearted.
Must try harder.

THE STOLEN TAXI

Muir Sperrings

Officer dear, it's such the craziest, craziest thing. I was just starting out on my way to visit great Aunt Bellephany, who lives in Bury, near Greater Manchester, well - almost that is, and…

The question of her address? Of course mine too. Listen - please - first things first; I don't like to be rushed. Miss Bellephany Peters of - you know, I cannot quite recall whether there is a number on the door. What I do remember is, the large brass knocker on it in the shape of a dragon, which she had put there to ward off the evil air that surrounds all loiterers that pass by. Anyway, its number one, Sapphire Street, Bury, Greater Manchester, and mine is… must get it right… never sure of my post code… if you can hang on for a moment I think I might have a letter with my address on it… yes, here it is, Miss Daphne Marple, no relation… (chuckle); The Chestnuts, Banks Drive, Little Musgrave, Cumbria CA17 4PQ.

Now what was the other question? Oh yes, why have I three large greyhounds in the back. Fortunately; I happened to stumble across this absurd little wool shop not far from great Aunt Bellephany's - they only took me two months to knit up, not bad really, considering all things. They are my birthday gift to her.

Yes, yes why did I steal this taxi. It started as a thought that grew and grew, the nearer I came to it. You see… it is my most favourite of colours… that was the start, and the more I walked round it looking at -everything… inside and out. I couldn't quite believe my eyes… there they were - the keys… a careless moment… a heaven sent chance… I dared myself.

SUMMER VISITORS

Sheila Lockett

In Hammamet, the pale sun was just appearing over the sparkling waters of the Mediterranean sea, sending early rays across the gleaming walls of the hotel that stood amongst bright flowers, green shrubs and towering trees; all kept in immaculate order by three permanent gardeners. Estelle Laudree drifted into the breakfast room early, it amused her to see the people who were booked on day trips stumbling bleary eyed from their morning wake-up call. She loved the precision with which the service was undertaken, waiters swiftly moving round the tables, their quiet voices asking "tea or coffee, Sir, Madame?" They removed the used crockery with a brisk efficiency or escorted favoured guests to their tables, always smiling.

Eh bien, Estelle thought, if it wasn't for this hotel being built, she didn't suppose she would be coming back year after year, to the place where her family home had once stood. Gazing at the sunlight flooding through the large windows, she remembered her dark womb-like home. Maman always kept the blinds drawn to prevent sun damage to her antique furniture, brought over with them on the ship from France. The coming of the war however had made all of that irrelevant, had changed their lives for ever.

In November 1942 the Germans, eager to step up their North Africa campaign, had arrived in Hammamet. General Rommel with his entourage moved into Sebastian Villa in the town and her father took an instant dislike to him. With a smile, Estelle heard again the outrage in her father's voice when the message came from M Petain, saying that the administration were to fully co-operate with the invaders.

Moustache bristling he had turned to his family.

"How dare he ask such a thing of us. We will do all we can to hinder these despicable Boche. I have seen the way they have treated our Jewish friends."

"What can one family do?" Estelle's brothers had said.

"There will be others who will stand with us against them," replied their father confidently, "and I will find those we can trust."

Moving into the foyer of the hotel, Estelle sat quietly in a corner, trying not to think of how different her life had been then. People crossed the marble floor, footsteps echoing, the harsh click of stiletto heels, the sharp slap of plastic flip-flops, and the soft shuffle of the leather shoes of the staff, as they advanced towards the doors ready to greet new visitors.

A skinny English woman, with a small pushchair holding a whining child, passed in front of Estelle, complaining to her husband in a loud Liverpool accent.

"This place is freezing, don't they have any heating?" She shivered in her thin strappy top. Sitting down she searched in her capacious bag for a cardigan.

Estelle looked towards the child who smiled at her; she gave a small wave which the child returned, his pearly teeth glowing in the cool darkness of the foyer.

Three women were waiting for their airport transfer. Snatches of their conversation reached Estelle.

"Hey, can you remember that guy who bought us the cocktails."

"What about you and that German bloke Chris, he was a bit of all right."

"Nah, too full of himself, right poser he were."

The two women looked at their friend. "Come on then Mo, haven't you got something to tell us."

"You don't know what goes on when your backs are turned."

"You sly cow, come on, give us the gen."

"As if."

The one called Chris punched her friend on the arm, her brash laughter baying out, striking a harsh note among the other tourists waiting quietly for the coach. The three returned to swapping stories, ignoring both Estelle and the other guests. Tanned and overfull with the sweet, sticky Tunisian pastries and the sugary croissants they had consumed for breakfast, they sat, folds of fat escaping under their short cropped tops and over the waistbands of their tight shorts.

It hadn't been like this in the Forties, Estelle thought. Not many people were overweight then, too little food and too many worries. Girls were modest, and they had manners, unlike today. She too had been modest, and when the war came had soon learned to be almost invisible. Clothes that did not draw attention to her figure, eyes downcast. Trying very hard not to be noticed by the German soldiers with their arrogant faces who strutted the streets of the town.

With a start, Estelle realised that she had missed seeing the coach pull up outside. A party of Germans were arriving to take part in a local competition, golf bags slung across their backs or pulled along, too precious to be entrusted to the hotel staff who followed, carrying suitcases. She knew she should forgive and forget, but why should she when memories of that far off time were still etched indelibly in her mind.

She stood up, the folds of her pretty, flower sprigged, blue cotton dress fluttering around her slim legs. Two youngsters in swimming trunks barged through the doors, heading for the outdoor pool and she slipped through behind them, smiling at their urgency.

Her two brothers had once been the same, young and confident. They had laughed at their father for wanting to hinder the occupying army, but within a few weeks of M Petain's announcement, her father had made contact with a local resistance group. The whole family were gradually drawn into covert action, fighting against the orders of their government. For the next few months, while trying to act normally, between them they managed to pass vital information on to the British forces when they eventually arrived in Tunisia.

Estelle's thoughts drifted back to the present, wishing her brothers could still be here enjoying the peaceful scene, wishing there had been no bomb to take their young lives, to devastate the family.

The pool, blue tiled and inviting, sparkled in the late afternoon sun. The boys jumped in and water droplets flew up, turning to shattered rainbows in the slanting rays of the sun. She smiled at their energy. God willing they would never know the anguish of war.

Estelle didn't mind being on her own now. She had grown used to the hotel, enjoyed the changing population. Occasionally she would see other women like her, sitting alone at the tables or by the pool. She would wonder why and make up stories about them, perhaps their husbands had died or left them for someone younger. Of course she would never intrude, or be so bold as to ask them about their single status. No, she had been brought up properly; it wasn't polite to be nosy. She knew all about the disadvantages of interfering.

A little girl of about three wandered across to where Estelle stood by the pool and clutched the hem of her dress. She looked down.

"Bonjour ma petite, ca va?"

"Tres bein Madame, merci."

The child reminded Estelle of herself, small, dark haired and earnest. The mother shouted at her daughter to move away from the edge of the pool. Veronique, the mother had called the child, a suitable name for a serious little girl.

With a smile and wink Estelle murmured "Au revoir, ma petite."

When she was Veronique's age she had lived on the family farm in Montigny. She had been twelve years old when her father had uprooted the family and brought them all to live in what was then the small town of Hammamet, not the big urban sprawl it was now with all the newly built resort hotels. It had been a culture shock, coming from the rich verdant forests of Normandy to this barren dusty land.

Estelle wondered what her life might have been like if her family had never left France. Perhaps she would have married a Norman farmer like her father, have had a daughter like Veronique, or boys like those still splashing about in the pool.

Time passed and the shadow of the hotel crept insidiously across the gardens. Gradually the children and their parents moved back indoors. Their shouting and laughter was replaced by chattering flocks of small birds, noisily claiming their favourite roosting places in the greenery climbing the hotel walls.

Hidden from sight and long since erased from memory, deep under the foundations of the Miramar Hotel, the bones of Estelle Laudree lay as they had since 1943. At the request of her grief stricken father, she had been buried secretly underneath the cellar of their house, by their friends in the Resistance. The pretty, flower sprigged, blue dress had long since disintegrated, as had the blood stains where the German bullets had torn through her frail body.

VAUGHAN WRITERS

Rose Aitken

Rose has been a prolific writer of short stories for more than six years. When she is not writing she is a member of the board of trustees for Vista, the primary service provider for people with sight loss in Leicester, Leicestershire and Rutland. She is also chairman of the Vista Forum and spends a lot of her time learning, reading and of course writing.

Wendy Edmond

Wendy was born in northern Gloucestershire, and has lived in several counties in the UK with her family before moving to Rutland. An eclectic range of jobs has included that of BBC minion, museum assistant, and regional manager in an international company. Since completing a Creative Writing course she helped to found Vaughan Writers, and is also a member of Rutland Poets. Among her interests are reading anything and everything, the cinema, and travelling - people watching (staring and eaves-dropping) proves to be a useful source of material for writing.

Jenny Evans

For the last six years Jenny has lived in the Market Harborough area with one geriatric cat, a very lovely husband, and a sense of humour. The husband and the sense of humour are essential, the cat appears to be everlasting.

Almost as soon as Jenny could string words together she started to compose rhyming verse. It was very important to her that the metre of these little ditties was correct and she spent many hours searching for that elusive 'right' word.

The fascination with rhyme continued into adulthood and evolved into the writing of fairy tale skits, which were performed by a local am-dram group.

By the time Jenny had completed the Creative Writing course at Vaughan College she had discovered a love of short story writing, something she hadn't even attempted since she was at school. This is probably the genre she now enjoys the most.

She is still writing poetry and this has progressed into what she has always thought of as grown-up verse – very little metre, and sometimes no rhyme at all. However Jenny does still occasionally lapse back in her old habits. After all,

If you've got the time

Then make it rhyme

Ann Fuchs

Ann has always enjoyed and admired the power of words. Her first attempt at writing was a booklet called 'How To Tret A Dog', sic. This manual, written at the age of five was in preparation for her greatest desire, her own dog to care for. She was not disappointed. Her enjoyment of A-level English and French did not gain good enough results for a literary career as she became diverted by the excitements of Bristol's glamorous social life.

After work, marriage and children, whilst at the same time moving around the UK, prompted by her husband's promotion, they made their home in Leicestershire. At this point, involved in local politics, her forte was writing political speeches and then latterly, publicity material and charitable funding applications working for the Fuchs Foundation, an education charity.

She joined Vaughan College's creative writing course in 2003 in order to learn the craft of writing and then embark on a novel based on her grandmother in law's inspirational diaries. This is yet to be achieved, but she has contributed short stories and poems to the publications of the University of Leicester's Vaughan Papers, entitled 'Off the Wall', and 'Our Leicester'.

C W Greenwood

C W Greenwood has been writing for over 30 years – a mixture of fiction, journalism and academic papers and books. The main subject areas have been international politics, history and psychological explorations, especially the combination of these within fiction. C W attended Vaughan College's Creative Writing course and wrote two short stories for Vaughan Writers' award-winning first anthology Against the Wall. The latest piece of work is 'The Secret' which is presented in this new anthology.

Roy Iliffe

One of the first books Roy C. Iliffe gratefully received as a Christmas present was 'Animal Farm' by George Orwell but its true significance didn't dawn upon him until years later. Indeed, he thought comedy and satire were more interesting and entertaining than reading for a degree in Politics at Swansea University. 'What the Butler Saw,' a Joe Orton play at the Phoenix Theatre in 1976 inspired him to enter the wonderful world of theatre and he has written, directed and acted in stage plays for over thirty years. He has also had poetry published, influenced by studying W.H. Auden at 'A' level English Literature, and taken a keen interest in stand-up comedy from Peter Cook to Stewart Lee. With regard to the latter a definite "Brucie bonus" has been the Leicester Comedy Festival and opportunities to perform at the Edinburgh Festival Fringe with Herrick Theatre.

He found the Certificate in Creative Writing course at Vaughan College a stimulating experience and time to reflect upon possible new directions. Thus, after much deliberation, his aim is to develop a comic prose style and join General Martin Amis's literary army in the never-ending war against cliché.

Sarah Ingram

Since Vaughan Writers' first prize-winning anthology and the birth of her daughter, Evie, Sarah shoehorns writing between motherhood and her professional occupation. Sarah's work is influenced by an early love of ghost stories and is inspired by all things Orcadian.

Sheila Lockett

Sheila's first success in creative writing was in junior school when she won five bars of chocolate in a school project competition. As rationing was still in place, this was a great treat and suddenly everyone wanted to be her friend.

After studying for certificate courses in Local History, Archaeology and gaining a BA degree, all of which consisted of writing numerous essays, Sheila felt she should now write for pleasure.

Since completing the Creative Writing Certificate course at Vaughan College which covered many differing genres, Sheila has had several short stories and poems published. She has also been short listed and runner-up in competitions, and who knows, that elusive first prize may be just around the corner.

Hobbies such as bell-ringing, singing in a local choir, tai chi, archaeology and family history all help to inform her writing.

Muir Sperrings

Muir really only found out that writing was for her, when she read out a short eulogy that she had written, at an Aunt's funeral three years ago. It was well received, and now having just completed an enjoyable two year creative writing course at Vaughan College is still putting pen to paper to compose.

Most of her inspiration comes from a love of the countryside having spent a childhood living out on the Somerset Moors and then later in life exploring the many bridleways of Leicestershire on her dear horse. Muir now lives on the edge of the City, in a converted flat in a Victorian Terrace House, complete with turret.

Working life had been spent in various occupations from looking after Polo Ponies at Windsor Castle, to having her own small clothing alterations business here in Leicester. Now retired, Muir still finds the time in between writing to crochet, paint, sew and another love - Bridge.

Eva Ziebicki

Eva joined Vaughan Writers a year after the group was formed, after graduating from the Creative Writing Course at Vaughan College. A background in teaching Drama and English in Secondary Schools in Leicestershire, coupled with current work with Primary School children for whom English is a second language, has influenced her writing interests.

Other pastimes include writing plays, previous directing and acting with a local Theatre group, Herrick Theatre. Eva has also performed at Leicester's Guildhall and at the Edinburgh Fringe Festival.